FROM THE GROVES OF ACADEME TO TERROR IN THE STREETS . . .

That was George Kirkham's harrowing journey, when he handed in his professorial robes for a uniform, a badge, and a gun.

From that moment on his life was a series of icewater shocks and illusion-shattering experiences—a life of excitement, of fear, of potential death in every on-duty moment.

"A SHOCKER . . . absorbing and thought-provoking."
                                        —*Publishers Weekly*

"AN EXCITING, NO-NONSENSE RECITAL."
                                        —*Pittsburgh Press*

"ENTERTAINING . . . INSTRUCTIVE . . . MOVING."
                        —L. H. WHITTEMORE, author of
                        The Super Cops

SIGNAL ZERO

George Kirkham

BALLANTINE BOOKS • NEW YORK

Library of Congress Catalog Card Number: 76-5426

ISBN 0-345-25771-5

This edition published by arrangement with J. B. Lippincott Company

Manufactured in the United States of America

First Ballantine Books Edition: July 1977

For Merry Ann, Craig, Kirk and Ben
and
for America's police officers

CONTENTS

A NOTE TO THE READER

THIS is the story of a university professor who left his campus for several months to work as a street patrolman in a large American city. It is my story. I do not pretend that what follows is an objective book about either the police or crime in our society. This could never have been such a work, although in the beginning I had thought that it might be. But what happened to me in those months made it impossible for me ever again to view a policeman's world from the detached perspective of a social scientist. I realize that now.

What follows is an account of the things I saw, felt and did during the time I worked behind a badge and uniform. It is neither a polemic written in behalf of the police nor a diatribe against them. It is simply the story of a group of remarkably ordinary men whose unfortunate distinction is that they must regularly function in the face of extraordinary human stress, and sometimes in the face of indescribable human tragedy.

The identity of the actual police department and city in which this drama unfolded is not important. The fact that it actually happened is. I have changed the sequence and some details of certain events, and have altered the names, descriptions and physical characteristics of all persons and places involved in them, in order to protect the privacy of those who made this book possible. Beyond that, I have tried in writing it to honor a promise I once made, to "tell it like it is."

George Kirkham

1

THE PROFESSOR

I suppose the whole thing really began on my first day of class as a newly appointed assistant professor of criminology. I was barely able to contain my enthusiasm as I entered the lecture hall and walked to the podium. For a time it had seemed as if the agonies of graduate school might last forever, but here I was at last, a Ph.D. with my own students and classes. As I watched the room full of undergraduates, I wondered if the new three-piece tweed suit I had bought for the occasion made me look professorial.

"Good morning. I'm Dr. Kirkham and this is Criminology four forty-seven: The Police and Society," I said. I could hear the sound of shuffling feet and opening notebooks as I turned and wrote my name and the course title in large letters on the board. After taking care of the administrative details of calling roll and passing out course outlines, I settled into my first lecture.

"I want to begin our discussion of the police and society today by examining a most important topic—one that will occupy our attention in lectures and reading throughout much of the quarter. I am referring to the subject of 'police personality.' " I paused for a moment to let my words take effect. "We're going to begin our analysis of police personality by considering some of the ideas of a man who is generally recognized as one of the

nation's leading experts on the subject. I am referring to
the author of your text, N. Lyman Thornton."

Of all the eminent criminologists I had studied under
during my years at Berkeley, Professor Thornton had
unquestionably impressed me the most. Nearly sixty-
five and in failing health when I first enrolled as a graduate student in one of his seminars, Thornton was the
author of a great many books and countless articles
about the police. On the eve of his retirement he was
still a much-sought-after professional witness in major
legal cases involving the abuse of police power, and various state and federal task forces on crime and the police often requested his assistance and counsel.

Probably the most impressive of all the scholar's lectures and writings were those that dealt with what he
believed was the relationship between what he called
police personality and patterns of police violence and
aggressiveness. The issues which he raised so often and
so eloquently in class sparked the interest and concern
of those of us who were his students at Berkeley during
the late sixties, those dark days of confrontation between student protesters and the police. First there had
been Mario Savio and the Free Speech Movement, then
the People's Park demonstrations and the Vietnam war
protests, among others. Violence and chaos became
realities of daily life at Berkeley from which none of us
were immune, not even Professor Thornton. I remember how once, as I sat in class listening to him outline
his plan for creating an unarmed American police
modeled on the British system, a chunk of cinder brick
came crashing through the window. Moments later a
bearded young man rushed into the room shouting,
"Power to the people!" He was quickly followed by two
policemen in riot gear who wrestled him to the floor
and handcuffed him.

I had watched the spectacle with a sense of loathing.
Fascists, I said to myself as I watched the two khaki-
clad policemen drag the youth outside. They embodied
the tradition of entrusting authority over other people's
lives to those least competent to exercise it. My anger

mounted as I thought of the riots in places like Watts, Newark and Chicago, and the then recent shootings of students at Kent State University by national guardsmen. I realized that it all came back to the nature of what Professor Thornton described as the police personality. He had spent most of his professional lifetime developing scientific support for the thesis that police work naturally attracts men who are basically insecure, hostile and authoritarian. Such individuals, in turn, he felt, use the power of their badge and uniform as a tool to bolster their own personal sense of adequacy at the expense of others—predominantly the poor and socially downtrodden. Professor Thornton believed that the answer to the problem of police personality was careful screening of the kinds of people who became policemen, to create through meticulous selection an elite force of officers consisting of only the most phychologically stable, best-educated and most compassionate members of a society, men whose professional aim would be solely to help and protect their fellowman, men who would not need the power symbolized by a gun or nightstick. He felt that, given the existence of such forces across the country, most of the problems associated with today's police would quickly evaporate.

I looked at the class. "First, let's consider the basic elements which Professor Thornton feels make up the so-called police personality." I picked up a piece of chalk and walked to the board. The students' pens began copying the list I wrote in anticipation of its likely reappearance on a future examination.

1. Authoritarianism
2. Chronic suspiciousness
3. Pessimism—cynicism
4. Hostility—extrapunitiveness
5. Personal insecurity
6. Physically aggressive reactions to stress stimuli
7. Political conservatism
8. Prejudice—racism

"There are, of course, other things," I said, "but these are the essence of what contemporary scientific research suggests are the hallmarks of the police personality. Quite a number of researchers have found evidence of those traits among the policemen they interviewed and administered personality instruments to." I pointed to the board. "The question I would like to consider today is this: Given the existence of police personality, do policemen become hostile, authoritarian and all the rest as a result of the nature of their work—the occupational stresses, in other words—or are they basically this way to begin with? Does anyone have an opinion on this point?"

I scanned the faces in front of me. There was a hand in the second row. "Yes?"

I looked at the man. He was tall and lean with a swarthy complexion and a drooping Zapata moustache. A little old for a student, I thought to myself.

He sat studying the list on the board for several moments before speaking. "Well, Professor, I believe that what you call a police personality, to the extent that it exists, has to be explained in terms of the kinds of things a policeman's work involves," he said.

Several students in the front row turned in their seats and looked at him.

"You don't feel, then, that the job itself just naturally attracts a certain kind of person, someone who's more insecure and hostile to begin with than the average person?" I asked.

"No, I don't," he replied. As I looked at the man, my eye was caught by a long scar that ran for perhaps two inches down the middle of his right cheek.

"I see. Then are you suggesting that anyone who becomes a policeman will automatically begin to take on the characteristics we've listed on the board—regardless of how personally stable and well educated he might be?" I asked.

"Yes, I believe so—providing, that is, that you place him in a rough enough assignment, say, policing a high-crime area, and keeping him there long enough. Even

Christ himself would come away screwed up!" There
was a ripple of laughter across the room as he continued. "And, Dr. Kirkham, I think you're making a value
judgment about all the traits you've listed on the board
as being undesirable," he said.

"Really?"

"Sure. For example, I'd argue that for a policeman to
be chronically suspicious of other people just makes a lot
of sense when you stop to consider the kinds of situations he runs into. The same thing is true about being
physically aggressive and authoritarian in lots of situations. He has to be!"

I smiled as I put my glasses back on. "Well, Mr.—?"

"Cagan. Frank Cagan."

"Yes. Well, Mr. Cagan, let me say that you're something of an environmentalist," I said.

The dark eyes looked at me. "Not really, Dr. Kirkham," he said. "I'm just a cop."

That was the beginning of my relationship with
Frank Cagan, a relationship that was to change my life
in ways I could not have imagined then. There were a
great many similar exchanges between us as we dis-
cussed Dr. Thornton's theories of police behavior
throughout Criminology 447 that quarter. Many of
these spilled over into heated debates lasting an hour or
more beyond the class period itself. Despite the fact that
we disagreed on almost everything when it came to the
subject of the police, I grew to like the tall policeman.
He had a good mind, and I tried more than once to per-
suade him to resign from the police department from
which he was on leave and pursue an advanced degree
in criminology.

He stopped by my office late one afternoon just after
final exams. "You know, I graduate in a few days," he
said. "I thought I'd try and buy you a beer before I
shove off."

We walked to a small pizza parlor a couple of blocks
away and slipped into a back booth.

"How have your other courses gone this quarter?" I

asked as a waitress brought us two glasses and a pitcher of beer.

"Not bad," he said. "I've maintained around an A-minus average all the time I've been here."

"That's remarkable," I said. I remembered that he had made one of the highest grades in my Police and Society class. I sipped my beer. "Tell me, Frank, have you enjoyed the criminology program?"

Cagan studied the glowing ash of his cigarette. "You really want to know?"

"Yes, of course."

"Well, Professor, to tell you the truth, I think most of it has been pretty much bullshit," he said.

"How can you say that about courses that you've obviously done well in?" I asked.

"Oh, sure," he said, "I study hard. I've learned how to play the game like everybody else, but as far as I'm concerned it's been one big waste of time and energy." He looked at me solemnly. "I'm going to level with you, Dr. Kirkham. Everything here—the professors, the books we read, the lectures you guys give—it's all so damn abstract and unreal to anybody who's ever seen what crime is really like. I just can't relate much of it to what's happening out on the streets."

We spent the next hour sitting there, drinking beer and rehashing a variety of issues we had debated during the preceding quarter. Cagan leaned forward as I flagged the waitress for another pitcher of beer.

"Professor, tell me something," he said. "Doesn't it strike you as just a little stupid that of all the faculty we've got teaching courses about the police at this university, not a one has ever been a cop? Not a damn one!"

I shrugged my shoulders. "So what?" I said. "Good Lord, Frank, I certainly don't have to be a burglar in order to study patterns of burglary, or a rapist in order to study the phenomenon of rape, do I? We're supposed to be scientists here. A scientist is supposed to maintain a certain distance from the things he studies. It makes for objectivity."

Cagan refilled our glasses. "You're missing my point, Professor. Being objective—being a scientist and all that crap—is fine, provided you've first got some basic understanding of what a subject is all about. But you guys lack that. Don't you see? You're completely isolated here from the whole business of crime and criminals. It's just one big intellectual game. Hell, I'll bet the average prof hasn't even bothered to talk to a cop in years."

"Now, just a minute. Whose fault is that?" I shot back. "You know as well as I do that every time a scientist gets within a block of a police station, every cop around freezes up. We can't get many of you people to talk to us even when we want to."

Cagan pointed a finger at me across the table. "I'm to tell you why that is, Professor," he said. "It's because we've about had a bellyful of being Monday-morning-quarterbacked by a lot of eggheads who never do anything but run around with tape recorders and give us idiotic questionnaires to fill out. Then they suddenly announce that they've just completed some earth-shaking study of police behavior. That gives them a license to sit back and criticize us."

"I swear you're a classic example of what Thornton means by the police personality." I laughed. "Paranoid as hell." My head was starting to buzz. I resolved to make the beer in front of me my last.

A grin appeared on Cagan's face as he leaned back in his seat. "You know something? I'd liked to see one of you high-powered intellectuals with all the answers just once put your money where your mouth is."

"What's that supposed to mean?" I asked.

"I'd like to see a criminology professor try it as a cop for a while. You know, put himself down in the gutter with the rest of us poor inadequate slobs who have to try to hold things together. I really wonder how much better a job one of you could do."

I laughed.

"You think that's funny?" he said.

"Not funny. More like ridiculous," I replied.

"What's so ridiculous about it? You kept telling us all quarter long about old Thornton's theories, about what swell cops well-educated, emotionally stable people would make. So why not take a crack at it yourself? I think it would make one hell of an interesting experiment, don't you?"

"No, I don't."

"Why not?"

"Frank, you know as well as I do that what you're talking about wouldn't be anything like a scientific experiment. If one of us were to become a cop in order to study things like crime and the police, he'd be far too personally involved in his subject matter. There would be too many uncontrolled variables, too many—"

"Oh, yeah, I forgot," he interrupted. "Don't ever let yourself get too close to reality."

"Come, now. What you're talking about would be completely meaningless," I insisted.

"Why? You said yourself in class that sociologists and psychologists are starting to enter all kinds of groups to study them—addicts, hippies, homosexuals. Hell, anthropologists have been going into other societies and mixing with the natives for years, learning their language and problems. I think you called it participant research, didn't you?"

"Participant-observation research," I corrected.

"So what's so far out about the idea of a criminologist studying cops the same way?"

"Well—" I searched my mind for a reasonable answer. "Frank, you know as well as I do that no police administrator in his right mind would ever consent to something like that, letting one of us become a cop in his department. It's crazy!"

"I'll bet you're wrong," Frank said. "I'll just bet our chief would go for it. By God, I'll bet the old man would." He paused, then continued thoughtfully, "Suppose he would. Let you work as a street cop in our department, I mean. Would you be willing to take a crack at it? You're still young enough."

"You don't think one of us could make it as a policeman, do you, Frank?"

"Nope. At least not without changing about ninety-five percent of your attitudes. Not without becoming a police personality." He laughed. "Hey, I've got just the beat for you! Ninety-five. I swear I'd give my right arm to see you down there in a uniform for a few months!"

"What's Ninety-five?" I asked.

"It's the worst beat in our city. I guess you'd say it's a fairly typical downtown slum. Street crime up to here—muggings, shootings, cuttings about every night. Real nice place. You know, lots of cheap bars, pool halls, flophouses. It's all black."

"Good heavens"—I scowled facetiously—"it must be a dangerous place!"

He looked at me with a serious expression on his face. "You may think it's a joke, Professor. I don't. One of my best friends was killed down there a couple years ago," he said. He traced a forefinger along the deep scar on the side of his face. "You see this? I got it in Ninety-five one night."

"What happened?" I asked. I had wanted to ask him about the scar but never had.

"I hadn't been out of the academy too long. It was a bar-fight-in-progress call. You get a million of them on a beat like Ninety-five. Anyway, when my partner and I walked in, there was this guy with a broken bottle in his hand. Drunk as hell. I decided I'd be a hero and take it away from him like they're always doing on TV. Even when he came at me with it, I still didn't use my stick or gun. I didn't want to hurt him. A real humanitarian," he said sarcastically. "It damn near cost me my right eye. I guess he might have killed me if it hadn't been for my partner. I should have blown his ass away." Frank stared off across the room.

It amazed me how easily the imagery of violence came to his mind. But then, I reminded myself, physical aggression was one of the characteristics of the police personality.

"Frank, don't you really believe that policemen

working in areas like your beat Ninety-five bring trouble on themselves much of the time?"

"How?"

"I mean by being overly aggressive, by overreacting to situations instead of approaching them rationally and objectively."

He shook his head. "Well, Professor, I could sit here all afternoon telling you war stories about Ninety-five and beats like it, but I'm afraid you'd still wind up believing what you want to."

I sat studying the half-empty glass in front of me. "All right, Frank," I said. "Let's say—just for the sake of argument—that I took you up on it, became a regular full-time policeman in your city for a while. Let's even say that I went to work in Beat Ninety-five. Do you really think that it would make any difference in the way I feel about the police, about crime?"

"Dr. Kirkham"—Cagan leaned forward and spoke in a low voice—"if you did that and didn't come back a changed man, I'd personally eat every book that Lyman Thornton ever wrote about the police!"

I laughed as I imagined Frank gnawing on Thornton's *The Police and Society* while glancing sideways at a stack of a dozen equally thick paper delicacies. To this day I'm not sure whether it was just the beer or whether Cagan's criticism of academic criminologists began to get to me. Anyway, his proposal started to intrigue me. "You really think it would be possible to do something like that, do you? I mean, for one of us—a social scientist—to become a policeman for a while?"

He lit another cigarette and I refilled our glasses.

"I don't see why not, providing you could meet the same requirements as any other recruit. Say, you're not really thinking about it, are you?" he said.

"Why not?" I smiled. "Can you think of a better way to establish the validity of the things I've been saying about the police in class?"

He looked at me. "You must be kidding," he said.

"What do you mean? It was your idea, Frank." I found myself filled with a sudden sense of elation.

"What's the matter? Does it worry you that one of us bubble-headed intellectuals might just go out and do your job our way with better results?"

He shook his head. "No. But wouldn't it bother you to have other people think of you as hostile and authoritarian, as a jackbooted storm trooper—a pig?"

"No, Frank, it wouldn't, and I'll tell you why." I held a forefinger unsteadily in front of his face. "Because I'm not any of those things, and I never could be. As I've said so many times in class and as you should know by now," I continued, "a man's personality is firmly established early in life by the kind of education and socialization he's exposed to. My way of viewing and dealing with other people wouldn't change just because I became a cop. I'd still be the same George Kirkham, just transplanted to a different role and environment."

"You think so, huh?"

"Absolutely, and I'm willing to prove it," I said. I stood up and prepared to leave. "Now, Frank, old buddy, it's your turn to put up or shut up. You can either go back and talk to your chief about the idea, or we can just forget the whole thing."

"I'll talk to him." He grinned.

I walked home slowly and unsteadily that night, chuckling to myself at the thought of having turned the tables on Cagan. Either I would never hear from him again or he would call me with the humbling disclosure that his chief of police had balked at the idea. Either way I would win, I thought, as I made my way up the steps leading to my house. Only the fact that my wife, Merry Ann, was asleep when I tiptoed into our bedroom kept me from telling her of my triumph. My sleep that night was uncommonly sound.

2

THE EXPERIMENT

"HELLO, Professor Kirkham? Please hold for Chief Benjamin," the telephone operator's voice said. Several days had passed since my meeting with Frank Cagan.

"Hello, my name's John Benjamin," a man's voice said after several seconds. "One of my men tells me that you're interested in coming to work over here for a while as a patrolman. Is that right?"

It took a moment for the words to register in my mind. "Uh . . . one of your men?"

"Yes, Frank Cagan. He's been going to school over there on an educational leave."

"Oh, of course, Cagan!" I put down the examination paper I had begun grading. "He mentioned he was going to say something to you when he got back," I said awkwardly.

Silence.

"Well, anyway, you see Frank and I were talking and we just started kicking around the idea that it might be really interesting if one of us here at the university were to spend some time actually working as a policeman. You know, in order to study certain ideas and theories about police behavior more closely."

"I see," he said. "You mean as a full-time uniformed patrolman, not as an observer?"

"Right. I guess that must sound pretty outrageous to you?"

"I think the idea might have some merit. How soon can you get over here to discuss it further?" he asked.

"Uh, well . . ."

He wasn't serious. He couldn't be. They must be trying to back me down, Cagan and this man Benjamin. That was it. I decided, since Cagan had obviously decided to pursue the point, that I would be the one to call *his* bluff.

We agreed on a date and time for our meeting, and a few days later I found myself on a plane headed toward it. Frank Cagan was waiting to meet me at the airport when I arrived. I very nearly didn't recognize him in the dark blue uniform he wore.

"I wasn't sure you'd show up," the policeman said as we shook hands.

We walked to a black-and-white police car parked at the curb. As I slipped into the front seat, it suddenly occurred to me that this was the first time in my life I had ever been inside a police car. An ominous-looking shotgun was locked in a metal rack against the dashboard directly in front of my knees.

A few minutes later we were cruising through the city's downtown area on our way to the police administration building and our meeting with Chief Benjamin. I watched the passing streets out my window. I knew a little about the city. It was a major seaport, an industrial metropolis of over a half million people. From my past conversations with Cagan, I knew that the city I was in suffered from most of the social ills that plague modern American society: high crime rates, poverty, deteriorated housing, and a large impoverished black population, most of it concentrated in and around the area that Cagan had described as Ninety-five.

On the way downtown, Cagan told me a little about the man who was his chief of police. Benjamin had headed the thousand-man force for almost fifteen years, he said. He was a controversial man, a cop's cop, old-fashioned. Tough yet progressive, scrupulously honest, deeply religious—yet subject to notorious bursts of profanity.

The chief was a big man, but otherwise he was not what I had expected. A pair of black horn-rimmed glasses, coupled with the silver moustache above his upper lip, gave him the appearance of a banker or a lawyer. He didn't waste any time getting to the point. "Just how serious are you about this, Professor? I mean about becoming a policeman."

I looked at Cagan. "Well, truthfully, I don't know. I do agree with Officer Cagan here that it would certainly be an interesting way to test a number of hypotheses about police attitudes and behavior that have appeared in recent years."

Benjamin sat studying me as I went on.

"Chief, let's lay our cards on the table, shall we?" I said. "However willing I might be to try an experiment like this, I find it a little hard to believe that you'd actually consider letting someone like myself become a policeman."

Benjamin frowned and rubbed the freckled skin on his forehead. "Well," he said, "there would be problems—lots of problems."

Now he was going to tell me that the whole idea was as impossible as it was absurd.

"We couldn't pay you anything," he continued. "There'd be all sorts of civil service and insurance problems to work out. You'd have to meet the same requirements as any other recruit—background investigation, physical exam, polygraph, training, the whole ball of wax."

He spent the next fifteen minutes describing in what I thought was discouraging detail the various procedures I would have to go through in order to become a police officer in his department. Then he surprised me by saying, "But if you're nuts enough to give it a try, and if you can meet all the requirements, I'm willing to put you to work as a patrolman down in Ninety-five."

We stood and walked to the door.

"Think it over," he said. "Let me know what you decide."

"I will," I said as we shook hands. "But tell me something, Chief."

"Shoot."

"I still can't understand why you'd consider letting me do something like this. Letting an outsider in. Surely you must—"

"Oh, I realize I'd be taking a chance, Professor."

"Then why?"

"Probably for a couple of reasons," Benjamin said. "One of them could be that I'm getting old and careless. But I'll tell you something, Dr. Kirkham. As corny as it might sound, I'm pretty proud of this department and the men in it. I don't think we've got a damn thing to hide from you or anybody else. Hell, I'm not naïve enough to think that we could keep you from seeing our dirty linen. If you come, you'll see some bad cops— men who never should have been allowed to pin a badge on. We try to weed them out. Usually we do, sooner or later. Sometimes we don't. But you'll see a lot more good cops in bad situations, men who keep on giving the job their best day after day. That's what I want one of you people to see, and there's really only one way you ever can." He walked across the room and stood in front of his desk. "I guess I still haven't answered your question, though, have I?"

I shook my head.

"It may surprise you to know," he began, "that a great many years ago I was a student at your university, studying criminology just like Officer Cagan here. You didn't know that, did you?"

"No, I didn't."

"It was pretty rough going back then," he said, "trying to pound a beat and get through school at the same time." He turned and smiled at Cagan. "That was back in the days when we didn't have educational leaves of absence, and when a cop got around on shoe leather instead of in an air-conditioned car. I used to sit in classes over at the university, dog-tired after working all night, and listen to guys like you talk about what a sorry bunch of cretins and bums cops are. You know, it got so after a while that I started feeling ashamed of being a policeman. I didn't want any of the other students to know."

He looked at me.

"Well, Dr. Kirkham, I promised myself way back then that if I ever got a chance to expose one of you people to a few of the realities of our job, I'd sure as hell take advantage of it—and here you are."

During the flight home that afternoon, I began to turn the idea over in my head seriously for the first time. Up until then the whole thing had been little more than a game I was playing with Cagan. It would be easy just to drop it, I told myself. Postpone the whole thing indefinitely. Yet, the more I thought about it, the more I was intrigued at the idea of trying something that no one in my profession had ever done before. And Benjamin's passionate sincerity had also impressed me. Why not try it? I thought. What better way to establish the validity of my ideas and theories than to put them into practice?

By the time the jet's wheels skidded to a halt on the runway, I had made up my mind at least to explore the idea further. I wondered, as I saw my wife and our ten-year-old son waving at me, how I would go about telling them—not to mention our friends and my colleagues—that at the age of thirty-one I was thinking about becoming a cop.

The next few weeks passed quickly. It was a time of intense ambivalence for me. I listened at length to the sound reasons for abandoning the idea that were offered by those around me. The whole thing was preposterous, impractical, unorthodox. Furthermore, despite the fact that I had already secured well over a hundred thousand dollars in government research grants as a beginning criminologist, I soon discovered that no private or public foundation would consider sponsoring such an outlandish project as I was proposing.

Probably the most persuasive of the arguments for giving up the whole enterprise came from my wife. We had just learned that she was pregnant with our second child. After struggling with me through the rigors of graduate school, she was just now beginning to enjoy the life of a faculty wife. After years of living in cramped apartments, we were finally about to build our dream home on seven acres of land in the country. To say that she responded to the idea of my becoming a policeman with something less than overwhelming enthusiasm would be an understatement. It was dangerous, she said. I was too absentminded. I wasn't cut out to be a policeman. How could we possibly afford it? What would it do to my career at the university? Was this what I had spent eight years in college and graduate school for? Despite the fact that I tended to agree with many of the points she raised, as the days went by I nonetheless found myself increasingly attracted by the idea of the experiment, by the personal and professional challenge inherent in it.

In the end, Merry Ann relented. If I was really determined to go through with this crazy plan, she would go along with it. Knowing this, I made the decision to press ahead.

The biggest single barrier immediately facing me was a relatively new state law requiring that every police officer and deputy sheriff successfully complete some three hundred hours of training prior to being sworn in and assigned to duty. Chief Benjamin's city was simply too far away for me to go through the department's own police academy and keep my job at the university at the same time. It soon became clear that the only way I could comply with the state law was to attend one of the certified regional police academies nearer my university on a part-time basis. This would mean that, in addition to carrying my normal teaching and administrative duties at the university, I could look forward to sitting in classes at the regional police academy four hours a day. Four hours a day, five days a week, for four solid months! The head of the police academy made it clear that, while they would be happy to accept me with Chief Benjamin's sponsorship, I would have to abide by

the same rules and regulations as any other recruit. I
would be immediately dropped from the program if I
missed more than three classes during the four-month
period or if I failed to complete successfully any phase
of the course. They would give me no special advan-
tages. It would be rough, I was warned, particularly for
someone trying to carry out the responsibilities of a full-
time profession at the same time. Most of the recruits in
the class would be in their early twenties. They would
be physically fit, athletic types for the most part. I
thought of the physical fitness and self-defense parts of
the training curriculum as he went over them with me. I
wasn't a physical person. My idea of exercise has always been to cut the lawn on a Saturday afternoon and
then relax with a cold beer. I was out of shape. No, I
told myself more truthfully, I had never been *in* shape.

My next step was to talk with Dr. Eugene Czajkoski,
our dean at the School of Criminology. While he admitted to having some reservations about my being able to
attend police school and meet my university responsibilities at the same time, he proved extremely cooperative
and supportive. Yes, he would see that my classes and
committee assignments were arranged in such a way
that I could start the academy next quarter. That being
accomplished, there was the question of just how long I
might be able to afford to work as a policeman—
assuming, that is, that I made it through the academy.
Merry Ann and I checked our savings book. Four
months at the outside. Maybe a little longer. That was
all the budget would bear, and I would have to be fru-
gal indeed or I couldn't stay away even that long. I
hoped it would be long enough to answer at least some
of the many questions about the police role that were
how beginning to fill my mind. I was excited. Summer
was not far away. I would plan on starting June 1,
1973. That would give me enough time to get through
the academy, and would also give Benjamin's personnel
division sufficient time to solve the bureaucratic problems involved in transforming a university professor
into a patrolman.

3

PAPER MAN

"PULL those shots down!"

The voice jolted me back to reality. Sergeant Daniel
Quinn continued shouting as he paced up and down the
line, his commands occasionally rising above the sound
of thirty-five revolvers firing simultaneously. It was the
end of my second month at the police academy.

"Come on! Let's go! You're running out of time,"
Quinn exclaimed as he stood behind me.

I fumbled with the gun's cylinder, and the empty
shells spilled onto the ground. I began reloading with
uncooperative fingers.

"Move, dammit!"

Only a few seconds left. I dropped into a crouched
position and thrust the weapon forward at waist level.
The paper man was an amorphous blur somewhere in
front of me. One. Two. Three. I counted the explosions
and kept on pulling the trigger as I squinted in the
bright sunlight.

"You're slapping the trigger! You're slapping the
trigger!"Quinn bellowed.

A moment later the range whistle sounded. The stac-
cato noise of gunfire was replaced by a numbing silence. Quinn stepped forward and tore my human silhouette target from its backing. "No good! Start
grouping your shots," he said as he handed it to me.

I looked at the range instructor's red face. Fiftyish.

Close-cropped hair. Loose-fitting military fatigues. A voice that rasped like sandpaper on gravel.

"All of you should be trying for gut shots! Like this," he said.

He clenched a fist and held it in front of his stomach. The rest of the class gathered around us as I surveyed the scattered pattern of holes in my target.

"But look," I protested. "I have one here in the head and two more in the chest."

"That's just fine," Quinn said. He took a handkerchief out of his back pocket and mopped his forehead as he examined my target again. "This kind of shooting is okay—okay, that is, as long as we're talking about a piece of paper. I've never known a one of these things to kill a cop."

"But any one of those three shots would have been fatal to a real person," I persisted. I was suddenly struck by the absurdity of the exercise, yet I reminded myself that killing the paper man was part of the game I was now playing. Having embarked upon it, I was determined to win.

Quinn turned toward me as he spoke. "What do you think would have happened if this sonofabitch had been real?" he asked. "Maybe coming at you with a gun or a knife?"

"Why, he'd be dead, of course," I replied.

Laughter came from the other recruits.

Quinn poked two fingers through the holes in my paper man's chest. "Yeah, he would probably die from either one of these, all right," he said.

"Then what's the problem, Sergeant?"

"The problem, Professor," Quinn began in an irritated voice, "is that he just might not have died until after he'd first killed you or somebody else." He raised his voice so the others could hear. "That's why we tell you guys to shoot for the gut. You hit somebody in the chest like the professor, here, and he might not stop. But a gut shot's different—it'll double him up, stop him cold right where he stands."

The professor, I thought. Quinn was now the only

one who called me that. To the rest of the instructors at the academy and the other recruits I had become "Doc" sometime during the past two months. At first the other men were plainly as uncomfortable with me as I was with them. However, time and the training process itself gradually began to push us into ever greater contact with one another. I began to connect names with faces, to exchange smiles and waves on the way to class. Whatever differences in age and education existed between us at the beginning, they seemed to become progressively less important as time went on. We became fellow sufferers in the ordeal of getting through the academy—drinking coffee together, joking, sharing notes on pending examinations, as well as hostilities toward instructors like Quinn who seemed determined to subject us to the most grueling experiences they could devise.

"What about my head shot?" I said. "It would have killed him instantly."

Quinn folded his arms and said nothing for a moment. "Yeah, it would have."

"Then—"

"It would have, that is, Professor, if you'd gotten lucky enough to hit him in the head. And that's just what it would have been—pure blind luck! In a situation like that," he went on, "you've got to allow for the effect of fear—panic." He looked at the other recruits. "I don't give a damn if you think you're Wyatt Earp. Take it from me," he said as he picked up one of the paper men, "if this bastard was real and trying to kill you, you'd be so scared you'd be lucky not to shoot yourself!"

Laughter.

"And you can forget all that Kung Fu and karate crap they're always using on TV," he said. "If and when it happens, you'll probably forget everything about self-defense you ever learned out here."

"So what do we do, Sarge?" one of the recruits asked.

He smiled. "Don't worry about it. You won't have time to think about it if it happens. You'll react automatically—like a robot. You'll just try to kill him before he kills you. It's wanting to stay alive that'll see you through. That's always the best thing you've got going for you."

I looked at him as he spoke. Quinn placed too much emphasis on policemen having to deal with violence and danger, I told myself. They all did. It was basically a social service occupation. I had once tried to explain to him how a number of studies have demonstrated that police work is statistically far less dangerous than jobs in agriculture, construction and mining.

"There were one hundred thirty-two policemen killed in the line of duty in this country last year," Quinn said. He took a gun from one of the recruits. "Ninety-five of them were killed with one of these things." He paused for a moment to let his words take effect. "Every one of those one hundred thirty-two guys had one basic thing in common," he said. "They all planned on going home at the end of their shift. Don't ever be ashamed of being scared when you get out there. In fact, make it a point to get scared and stay scared." He wiped his forehead with the handkerchief again. "You show me a street cop today who says he isn't scared every time he puts that uniform on and I'll show you a liar or a fool—either way, he's a dumb bastard that I don't want to have to work with."

He handed the recruit back his gun.

"The day you pin that shield on, you'll become a target for more punks and nuts than you can shake a stick at. It's too bad we can't make certain that somebody doesn't try to cancel your ticket until you've got a little experience under your belts—but the streets don't work that way."

I looked at the dark blue revolver in my hand as he continued speaking. I hated guns. I always had. I had dreaded the firearms phase of the course more than any other. As Quinn went on I remembered the feeling of horror that had gripped me the first time I fired the gun. I had closed both eyes tightly, then bit my lower lip as I squeezed the trigger. After what seemed like an eternity the alien object had finally recoiled in my hand with a loud noise. That initial fear had quickly passed, however, much to my surprise. In time, shooting the paper man became easy and natural, sometimes almost fun. Like Cowboys and Indians as a child. It was a harmless enough game to be playing when you got right down to it, I told myself, and I began looking forward to our afternoons at the range, if only for the relief from classroom exercises which they brought.

"Okay, everybody, now listen up!" Quinn said.

We all formed a semicircle around a police car that had been driven onto the outdoor range for the next exercise.

"Now we're going to move on to some combat situations involving the shotgun," he said.

Combat? Had he actually said "combat"? Quinn's warlike conception of the police mission never ceased to amaze me. And now shotguns! How many times had I said in criminology lectures that the police have no business carrying offensive weapons like shotguns? As if handguns weren't bad enough. I thought of Lyman Thornton's plan for an unarmed police in the United States. An armed and violent police force makes for an armed and violent citizenry, he had said.

"Professor."

I turned toward Quinn.

"You and Eason come on up here," he said.

I joined a tall recruit with curly blond hair beside the police car.

"Now here's the picture," he began. "Let's assume that you two are a unit that's just rolled up on a robbery in progress. Eason, you drive. Professor, you be the passenger officer. When I blow the whistle, I want you two to pretend that those three bad guys over there have just opened fire on your car." He pointed at three human-silhouette targets some yards to the front and left of the police car.

Cops and robbers, I thought to myself. How melodramatic.

"Professor," Quinn said, "you'll get the shotgun out

of the rack and take up a position firing over the hood. Eason, you'll fire your service revolver from behind the trunk. Got it? Stay low, now. Watch your cover."

I nodded unenthusiastically. More paper men. The average policeman never fires his gun in the line of duty. So why bother with all this nonsense? I asked myself. The shrill sound of Quinn's whistle interrupted my thoughts.

Eason began scrambling out from behind the wheel to confront our paper assailants while I pressed the release button on the shotgun rack. The riot gun's short barrel dropped back into my grip. I held it in both hands and got out of the car.

"Dammit, Professor, get down! You're giving them a target," Quinn shouted.

In my haste I tripped over something and fell across the police car's hood with a dull thud. I could hear the sharp report of the other recruit's revolver as I groped with my right hand for the shotgun's safety release. More shots. Where on earth was the release? Was it on the left or the right? Perhaps the bottom.

Eason stopped firing to reload.

"What the hell are you doing out there, Professor? Your partner's gun is empty and you still haven't fired a shot!"

Crude. Quinn was really about the crudest person I'd ever met, I told myself. Ah! I finally felt my finger on the safety just as the range instructor unleashed a string of curses. I racked the first round of twelve-gauge birdshot into the chamber and took aim at the paper robber nearest me. I squeezed the trigger. Take that, Quinn! The deafening blast reminded me that I'd forgotten to put my earplugs on. Damn! The first paper robber shredded and I swung the barrel across to the next one as I heard Eason begin firing his revolver again. Tiny pops were punctuated by the shotgun's roar. The weapon recoiled again against an already sore shoulder as I found myself wishing that I had more natural padding than 160 pounds could offer.

"Hurry, dammit! You think those guys are going to

sit back and wait for you?" Quinn called out as I racked another round.

I fired again. The last of the empty red shell casings tumbled onto the car's hood with a metallic sound. The third and final robber had been dispatched.

Quinn shook his head and looked at his stopwatch. "Christ, that's awful! Really awful," he said as Eason and I walked over to him. "If that'd been for real, you'd both be dead as hell!"

I stood there feeling the frustration build inside me. My shirt was soaked with perspiration. Quinn turned away from us and began criticizing our performance to the rest of the class. My ears were still ringing and my shoulder was sore. It was on days like this one that I told myself that I had had enough, that I was going to quit. I went home that night in a black mood.

But I didn't quit. For some perverse reason I remained with the class of recruits as it moved on to other lessons. It was strange: delivering lectures to classes at the university in the mornings, then rushing to the police academy to play student myself. Poetic justice, I once thought to myself. I must have given lectures that were as boring as some of those I now had to listen to. Still, it was a peculiar sensation to find myself on both ends of the educational system during a single day. For the first time in my long career as a student, I now found myself preoccupied with quite concrete—rather than abstract—issues and problems. Learning how to stop a car. Learning the procedures involved in properly securing a crime scene. Learning how to give court testimony. Learning how to interview suspects and witnesses. Along with my peers, I investigated imaginary traffic accidents, lifted latent fingerprints off objects, and practiced giving mouth-to-mouth resuscitation to a female dummy, whom we nicknamed "Babs" (and who was the subject of rather coarse humor at times). Many nights I went home and soaked my aching muscles in a tub of hot water after the experience of being repeatedly thrown on my posterior by uniformly stronger and younger recruits during self-defense training. And I wrote practice reports. Millions of reports, it seemed: robbery reports, burglary reports, assault reports, missing person reports, juvenile reports, homicide reports and a great many others that have mercifully escaped memory. Television policemen are rarely seen with a piece of paper in hand, but a real policeman's life, I began to think, must be utterly consumed by report writing.

Just as I was starting to believe that the miseries of the academy would last forever, I could glimpse the light at the end of the tunnel. The day of graduation was drawing close. I had successfully completed all the department's other requirements, even the polygraph or "lie detector" test, despite my anxious admission that I had experimented with marijuana during college (I later discovered that this is quite common among police applicants today). With the approach of graduation from the academy, I found myself looking forward to my coming career as a policeman with an enthusiasm that bordered on excitement. It would be a marvelous scientific adventure, I told myself.

One warm afternoon in May, I jammed the older of our two family cars with personal belonging and said good-bye to my wife and son. Yes, I would write and call regularly. I promised I would try to get home for a visit once every couple of weeks. Yes, of course, I would be careful. I looked at my wife as she stood there with tears in her eyes. She was large with the baby now. It was a bad time to be leaving, I thought, even though I could quickly fly home when she got close.

"Honey, really, the job's not all that dangerous," I assured her, as I started the car and waved good-bye.

4

ROOKIE

PATROLMAN 9027.

I studied the inscription on the surface of the badge with a sense of unreality. Ninety-twenty-seven. So that was me, I thought. I was finally a policeman. I pinned the badge to the dark blue uniform shirt and sat on my bed buffing one of the regulation black shoes to a high gloss, wondering what my first tour of duty would be like. I had been assigned permanently to the evening watch and found myself glad of it as I glanced out the window at a temperature sign atop another building. It registered a scorching 91 degrees. Even with the short sleeves and open collar of the summer uniform, it would still be hot and sticky until darkness eventually cooled the city.

I took the wide Sam Browne belt from the dresser and began positioning the required items on it: holster, handcuff case, ammunition pouch, a small aerosol can containing liquid tear gas. Then I removed the new Smith and Wesson .38-caliber service revolver from its box and wiped it with a clean cloth. Here it was again, I thought. A mute but inescapable symbol of violence that I would now be carrying every night for months. I loaded the gun and strapped it in the holster. "Violence, never forget, is the ultimate confession of inarticulateness." Professor Thornton had once said that. I smiled to myself. There was nothing inherently violent about the gun itself, or any other weapon for that matter. I slipped the nightstick into a metal ring on the belt. The good or evil of any inanimate object has to be measured in terms of the mind and personality of the man who possesses it, I told myself. No, I had nothing to fear from either the gun or the nightstick. They were dumb objects. They couldn't make me a violent person. It wasn't in my nature.

I stepped to the mirror and adjusted the uniform cap. It was amazing, really amazing, I thought, as I stared in disbelief at the reflection. I actually looked like a policeman! A little more slightly built, maybe a good bit older than the average rookie, but a policeman just the same. I walked to the apartment's lone window and looked out at the city. It was out there somewhere. The ghetto. The area that Frank Cagan had variously referred to as "the blocks," "the project," "the war zone." My beat, Ninety-five. I would see it tonight for the first time.

I opened the door and stepped into the hall. The air outside my room was musty and thick with the smell of smoke from a backed-up incinerator. I had thought the building might be on fire during my first new nights at the Hotel Raleigh, but I soon discovered that the smell was chronic. I made my way down the hallway. It was drab and depressing. A lone light bulb suspended from a long cord cast dim light on walls covered with years of unattended dirt. I knocked over a half-empty bottle of Annie Green Springs in the semidarkness. What a dump, I thought. Not a dump, the professor's voice within me corrected, a lower socioeconomic milieu.

I had taken a room in the Hotel Raleigh with great reluctance, and only because I couldn't afford any place better. Its rates and its proximity to the police station were perhaps the building's only redeeming features. Once touted as one of the most fashionable hotels in the downtown area, the Raleigh's physical appearance and clientele had both steadily deteriorated over the years in the face of urban progress. Now the high ceilings, baroque architecture, and boarded-up fireplaces were only vestiges of that time. Today, with the ghetto five blocks away, the Raleigh was only a step above a flophouse. Thieves and drifters. The poor. The elderly. Pimps and their prostitutes. The Raleigh's tenants were drawn to it principally by the flashing neon promise of GOOD RATES—DAY OR WEEK. I was glad Merry Ann couldn't see the place. I had falsely represented it to her on the phone as "modest but cozy." Cozy if you happen to be a roach, I thought, as I started down the creaking staircase. Although I had been living there for almost a full week now, as I went about the business of getting processed through the department's personnel division, I had managed so far to melt into its bleak landscape as easily as the other tenants. No one knew my name or what I did. No one cared. No one knew that I was—or was about to become—a policeman. Today was the first time I had worn the uniform in the building.

Several elderly men looked up from a checker game in the lobby as I entered it. Someone nudged an unkempt form that was snoring loudly in one of the room's several tattered chairs. The man righted himself and cursed.

"Is there trouble, Officer?" a woman's voice asked.

I turned as I felt her hand on my arm. Who was she talking to? "Uh . . . no, ma'am. Everything's fine. I live in the building," I managed. I smiled and touched the brim of my hat. My first encounter with the public, I thought to myself. I opened the Raleigh's front door and stepped onto the sidewalk. A nice evening. I would walk to the station tonight, I thought.

"Hey! Hey! Wait up a minute."

The voice came from behind me. I turned back toward the lobby and saw an old man in a wheelchair vigorously pushing himself forward.

"C'mere . . . I got something for you," he croaked. He beckoned me toward him.

I bent over and coughed. His breath was awful. "Yessir. What can I do for you?"

"See there? You see that right there?" he said. He pointed toward a black woman in her early twenties.

The woman was just starting up the staircase with a heavyset white man. She wore a blond wig piled high on her head and the kind of skirt known on campus as a micro-mini.

"Now that nigger bitch is whoring up there just as sure as hell!" he exclaimed. He propelled his chair to the foot of the stairs as the pair disappeared. I followed him. "I seen her go upstairs with three fellers today already. Here's her room number." He handed me a scrap of paper.

"Well . . . uh—sir—"

"I already checked it out. That's her room all right. You can catch her now if you just go on up," he said.

"Sir, the thing for you to do is to call the police department and ask for the vice division. Tell them your com—"

"Why I gotta do that?" he interrupted. "I just told you what I seen, didn't I? I don't want to get involved in no trouble. I just want that bitch arrested. Don't decent people in this place have no rights?"

"Yes, of course. But, you see, I don't have the authority to—"

"What? You're the law, ain't ya?" he said. "Why can't you arrest her? She's breaking the law. Any fool can see that plain and simple." He wheeled back across the room.

"It's not that easy. I'd have to have something more than—"

"Aw, just forget it," he said irritably, with a wave of one hand. "If the police ain't go no respect for the law, then I ain't neither."

I thought for a moment about trying to explain to him the legal requirements for an arrest, perhaps tell him something about the constitutional safeguards that protect an individual's personal liberty and privacy. No. I turned toward the door with a vague feeling of embarrassment. Several people in the lobby were staring at me. Could they tell I wasn't *really* a policeman? Had I betrayed myself already? I put the thought out of my mind and left the building.

I gradually fell into a relaxed stride as I watched the sidewalk cracks appear and disappear beneath my feet. I glanced sideways at a store window and caught the flash from the metal on my uniform. Walking policeman. The traditional cop on the beat. There weren't enough of them anymore, I thought. That was one of the things wrong with modern police departments. Policemen had become nothing more than blurs of passing light. Anonymous objects encased in steel, drifting silently and endlessly up and down the streets. Men who were seen only in times of trouble. No wonder the police were so often resented, so often despised. They were strangers to the very people they served. I wouldn't be that kind of policeman, I told myself.

I continued walking. Childhood images of the prototypical policeman drifted into my mind. A movie I had seen as a boy. Pat O'Brien. Whistling. Twirling his nightstick on a leather thong as he smiled at passersby. Plucking an apple from a fruitstand without paying. Patting towheaded children on the head as he walked his beat. Then I remembered the police at Berkeley during the demonstrations. Silent. Minatory. Clad in riot gear. Men with long sticks held rigidly across their chests. Faceless men.

A horn.

"Officer . . . say, Officer?"

I turned toward the voice. It was coming from a tired yellow station wagon that had just pulled to the curb.

"Hi. What can I do for you?" I piped. I walked over and leaned in the passenger window. A middle-aged man in a white T-shirt was seated behind the wheel. Two small boys gnawed on chicken drumsticks in the back seat.

"Tell him what policemen do to little boys who throw trash out of car windows." The man scowled. He turned in his seat to face one of the boys.

The child looked terrified as his eyes met mine. They darted to the gun at my side, then back to my face.

"Son," I began awkwardly, "don't throw things on the ground." I felt like some kind of ogre. The boy cowered in one corner of the car and continued watching me. I went on in my best Smokey-the Bear voice. "You see, when there's trash all over the streets, that means that somebody has to come and pick it up."

"You hear that, Albert?" the man interrupted as he glared at the boy. "You want me to let this policeman take you, huh? You want to get locked up?"

The boy started bawling. He moved to another corner of the car where he apparently felt safer from my reach.

"Thanks, Officer. Appreciate it," the man said without looking at me. The station wagon receded in a cloud of blue smoke.

Why did he have to do that? I thought as I continued walking. I remembered a poster I had once seen showing a policeman carrying a small child from a burning building. THE POLICEMAN IS YOUR FRIEND, it had said.

I paused at an intersection and waited for the WALK sign to begin flashing. Then it hit me. I felt a faint sense of panic. Which way was the station? I looked up and down the street. I was sure it was here. I looked around again. Good Lord! This is ridiculous, I thought to myself. I had driven by it at least twice during the past week. I remained on the corner for several minutes studying its landmarks. A check of the street guide in my back pocket provided no clues. I was standing there reflecting on my predicament when I noticed a young woman inside one of the shops watching me. I rocked on my heels and clasped my hands behind my back nonchalantly. I could ask her where it is, I thought. I'll bet she knows. I reproved myself angrily. Policemen aren't supposed to ask directions. They *give* directions. And whoever heard of a policeman who couldn't find his own police station? I resolved that I would rather wander the streets all night than ask anyone for directions.

I felt more than a little relieved when I was finally able to make out the shape of the police building after several more blocks. And not a moment too soon. I could hear thunder as I hurried up the front steps. It was starting to rain. Other figures in blue were beginning to emerge from the parking lot across the streets and walk quickly toward the building in the light mist of rain that was now falling. I glanced at my wristwatch. The evening shift I would be working with would be reporting for duty in a few minutes. I walked inside the station house and looked around. Yellow flaking plaster. A badly worn and discolored carpet covered with coffee stains. Broken windowpanes hastily replaced by pieces of plywood. Boxes of empty Coke bottles stacked high in one corner. The Raleigh's twin sister, I thought to myself. A large tabby cat regarded me as it yawned and stretched atop a cigarette machine.

I examined the assignment paper in my back pocket and approached the front desk. A balding man with sergeant's stripes and pendulous dark bags under his eyes sat eating a sandwich behind it.

"Pardon me, Sergeant, where can I find the Zone Three patrol commander's office?" I asked.

He looked up and gestured down the hall without saying anything. A number of uniformed men were milling around outside the downtown area patrol captain's office. Talking. Joking with one another. Drinking coffee. I felt relieved that no one seemed to notice my presence. Just another blue uniform, I thought to myself, pleased to have been able to carry my impersonation this far at least. I knocked on the closed door.

"Come in," a voice said.

The captain sat behind his desk chewing on a dry pipestem as he talked on the phone. "Sorry, Harry, but I can't spare you a man—not tonight," he said.

A portable radio on a table behind him blared occasionally as it scanned several frequencies. Another phone on his desk began ringing. He frowned at it momentarily but ignored it and continued talking.

A uniformed man came up and bent over the desk. The man spoke in a hoarse whisper. "Cap'n, some dumb sonofabitch just jumped off the Main Street bridge," he said. "Traffic's backed up all the way down to Twentieth already. We don't have a thing in service."

"Ah, hell! Hold a minute, Harry." The captain sighed as he cupped a hand over the phone's receiver. "Well, see if we can borrow something from Four Zone until some of our units break free," he instructed.

The man nodded and walked off as the phone conversation resumed.

"What do you need?" the captain said once he'd hung up the phone.

"Captain, I'm George Kirkham," I said.

He looked at me uncomprehendingly. "Yeah. So what do you need?"

I fumbled with the assignment paper and handed it to him. "I'm the criminology professor," I began hopefully. "The one who's going to be working in Ninety-five for a few months."

He read the paper. "You're the guy, huh? I just got a memo about it this morning," he said. He gestured toward the wooden chair in front of his desk. "Tell me something."

I nodded and smiled uncomfortably.

"Just whose bright idea was this—I mean, putting you down in Ninety-five?"

"My own," I replied. "I thought it would make an interesting experiment—"

"Experiment?" He laughed. "Mister, no offense, but you must have a wheel loose somewhere." He stood and walked over to a large map festooned with colored pins. He tapped his finger on a small, irregularly shaped square in the very center. "Ninety-five's the worst this city's got to offer. It's a beat for an experienced officer—not a rookie. Not even a rookie with a Ph.D.," he added.

"I can take care of myself," I said.

"It's not you I'm worried about," he replied. "It's the poor bastard I've got to put with you. Who's going to take care of him?"

"I've been through the same training as everybody else," I said. Then I added, "I finished in the top quarter of my academy class."

"Now that's just great! Hooray for you!" the captain said.

I felt my face flush with anger.

"The academy doesn't mean much out on a beat like Ninety-five," he said. He took a tobacco pouch from his top desk drawer and began filling his pipe. "If you go to work down there, you can forget around seventy-five percent of whatever you learned in the classroom. Forget it—that's my advice—and then get yourself the biggest damn stick you can find," he said.

Terror tactics. The tired danger mystique again, I thought.

"Don't get me wrong," the captain said. He lit his pipe. "I think what you're doing is great. I know some judges and probation officers I'd like to put out on the streets for a few days."

"Then—?"

"It's just that Ninety-five's not the place to try it," he said. "At least not to begin with. Maybe one of the suburban beats. We've got a ton of them out in Two Zone. Why don't you—?"

"Chief Benjamin has already given me permission to go to Beat Ninety-five," I said. "It's part of our arrangement."

He shrugged his shoulders. "It's your ass, not mine."

"That's right." I smiled.

We stared at each other for a moment.

"Go ahead and fall in with the others," he said. He took a uniform cap with gold braid from behind him. "I'll introduce you."

I filed into one of the rows of folding metal chairs in the back of the room as the other men came in. A few moments later the room came to attention. The captain walked in, followed by a silver-haired man wearing lieutenant's bars.

The lieutenant began calling the roll. "Alt."

"Here."

"You'll be riding Sixty-one—also covering Sixty-four. We're short again tonight," the lieutenant said.

The policeman named Alt groaned a protest as the lieutenant went on.

"Blake."

"Here."

"Riding Beat Fifteen. Castillo."

A husky Latin youth responded.

"Castillo, you've got Twenty-five. Dempsey."

"Here."

I sat uneasily in the chair as I waited for my name. It finally came."

"Kirkham."

"Here," I said in a voice that sounded too high to me.

"You'll be riding Ninety-five regularly," the lieutenant said.

Several of the men turned in their seats and looked at me. One whispered something to the man next to him. I could read nothing in the faces around me.

The gray-haired figure finished calling the roll. Then he said, "Fellas, the captain has a few words to say to you before we get into the daily bulletin."

The room became extremely quiet as the zone commander came forward and spoke. "Professor, stand up back there, if you will," he said.

I got to my feet.

"Men, this is Dr. George Kirkham. He's a criminology professor who's going to be working with us here in Three Zone for a while. You've probably heard about it already."

Whispering. Glances toward me. Everyone in the department would have to be told exactly who I was and what I was doing. Chief Benjamin had insisted on that as one of the conditions of the project. The men trusted him, he said. He wouldn't jeopardize that trust by trying to pass me off as an ordinary recruit, even though that might make my presence and acceptance easier. That was fine with me, I had said.

"As you can see from his uniform," the captain went on, "Dr. Kirkham is a fully sworn police officer in this department. During the time he's here, I expect you to treat him the same as you would any other officer. No better and no worse. He has the same authority on the streets as any of the rest of you, the same training."

Silence.

"I think we can dispense with the 'doctor' and 'professor' titles." He smiled. "If you wear this badge, you're just another cop as far as I'm concerned. You guys know me. I don't give a damn if one of you happens to be the chief's son-in-law, or Jesus Christ Himself, for that matter. If you're right, I'll go to the wall with you. If you're wrong, I'll hang your ass."

Laughter sounded across the room.

"It'll be the same way with Patrolman Kirkham back there."

I looked at him. That was fine, I thought. I didn't expect to be treated any different from the rest of them. I didn't want it, I told myself.

"Kirkham is really one hell of a lucky guy," he said. "Not only is he going to get to work Ninety-five on nights—"

"The men laughed.

"—but I'm also giving him D'Angelo as a partner. That means he's bound to see some of the sorriest excuses for professional policing we've got in this department." He grinned. There were hoots and catcalls around the room. He raised his hands in a gesture for silence. "It's all yours, Bill," he said to the lieutenant as he left the assembly area.

"Okay, men, listen up," the lieutenant said as a sergeant began handing out the daily bulletin. It contained a lengthy list of reported crimes in Zone Three for the preceding twenty-four-hour period, as well as descriptions of suspects and vehicles to be on the lookout for. "We've got a partial description on those two that hit Walt's Pawn Shop on Jefferson this morning," the lieutenant continued.

The men in blue began clicking ball-point pens and adjusting clipboards in their laps.

"Both suspects are black males in their early twenties," he began.

"Hey, can you imagine that, Al?" an officer in front of me whispered to the man next to him.

"Must be a mistake," the other man replied.

"Suspect Number One," the lieutenant went on, "around six-two. Two hundred pounds. Goes by the street name of Benjie. Plaited hair and a short beard. Last seen wearing . . ."

"Probably no more than a few thousand like that in the city," another policeman said.

"Both suspects were last seen in the Regency area early this afternoon. Reportedly driving a white-over-red sixty-five Mustang bearing a stolen plate. MNX-five-five-eight. That's Mike-November-X-ray-five-five-eight."

I wondered what the chances were that I might see the men or their car tonight. I jotted down the number and vehicle description in my pocket notebook.

"Consider these two guys extremely Signal Zero," the lieutenant said.

Signal Zero? I started to ask the man next to me what it meant just as the lieutenant went on.

"They scored a large supply of weapons and ammo from Walt's," he said, "including two M-one carbines and several forty-five automatics."

A black policeman down my row to the left whistled. "Hey, Smitty, keep the brothers off my beat, okay?" he said to someone.

The lieutenant finished the reading file, and the men began collecting flashlights and other pieces of equipment from beneath their seats. "Dismissed. Nail 'em and jail 'em," he said. "Oh, one other thing," he added as an afterthought. "I hate like hell to keep bringing this up, but we're still getting complaints about officers being out of their cars with no hats on."

"Shit!" the policeman next to me muttered to no one in particular.

"Put the damn thing on your head," the lieutenant said. "It just takes a couple of seconds and it makes us all so very proud of you. Dismissed."

The lieutenant motioned for me to come to the front

of the room as the men began filing out, laughing and talking with one another like so many schoolchildren. Soon only the lietutenant and another man remained in the front of the room.

"This is Ron D'Angelo. He'll be your regular riding partner for a while," the lieutenant said.

I looked at the man. He was big. Muscular. The broad shoulders stooped slightly as he stood and extended a hand.

"Glad to know you," he said as we shook hands. An accent. New York, I thought.

"Angie, the two of you will be riding permanent evening watch in Ninety-five for the next couple of months. Then we'll move you over to Ninety-seven and put Griffin with him. Okay?"

"All right by me." The big man shrugged. He took a cigar from a shirt pocket and began unwrapping it.

I looked at the creased face, the gray-and-black tufts of hair protruding from the sides of an otherwise bald head. The arms were tanned and massive; I could just make out the outline of a faded tattoo on the back of one of them. Hair squirmed from beneath the uniform shirt's open collar and a thick brush of moustache separated the upper lip from the large nose above it.

"Try to keep him out of trouble, Angie," the lieutenant said.

A smile flickered on D'Angelo's face as he wet the cigar and lit it. "Now, sir, you know me better'n that," he said. "C'mon." He turned toward me. "I'll show you where we check our gear out."

We stood in line outside a supply window for several minutes before checking out a portable radio, shotgun and shells from the man behind the counter.

"So you're a university professor, huh?" D'Angelo said.

It was raining hard now and we paused at the door of the station house to pull plastic raincoats over our uniforms.

"That's right," I replied. We walked down the steps and jogged quickly across the street toward a black-

and-white car parked at the curb. D'Angelo unlocked it and we got in.

"So what you doing out here?" he asked as he shook the rain from his cap. The cigar bobbed in one corner of his mouth as he spoke. I hope he doesn't smoke many of those things, I thought. It smelled awful.

"Well, I'm sort of doing a research project, you know, to see what I can learn about police work."

"Yeah?" He began shoving shells into the shotgun's magazine. "How much they paying you?"

The police radio came alive with conversation as he locked the weapon in its rack on the dash and turned on the ignition.

"Uh. . . . nothing. I'm not getting paid anything."

He turned toward me with a look of surprise. "You ain't getting no money for this?" He took the cigar out of his mouth.

I shook my head.

"You must be nuts!" he said. "Say, what do I call you, anyway?"

"George is fine. Or Doc," I said. "That's what they called me at the academy."

"Doc? Okay, I'll call you that," he said. "My real name's Ron, but 'most everybody calls me Angie." He took the radio's microphone from its clip on the dash and frowned as he sat with it in his lap. "Will you listen to that? It's getting so damn crowded you can't even get on the radio no more!" He waited impatiently for a break in the almost continuous stream of tranmsissions.

"Headquarters . . . Two Lima Ninety-five is in service. Be covering beats Ninety-five and Ninety-four," he said finally. "Officers D'Angelo, badge Twenty-two-nineteen, and—" He released the mike button. "What was your last name?"

"Kirkham."

"Kirkham. Badge Ninety-twenty-seven," he said as he craned his neck to read the number stamped on my shield.

"Ten-four, Two Lima Ninety-five," a woman's voice replied.

Well, here it is, I thought to myself as we pulled into the street: my first night. It was still pouring. The windshield wipers slapped the glass rapidly as we left the station. I was just about to speak when my eye was caught by something.

"Excuse me, but what's that you're wearing underneath your shirt?" I asked.

"What, this?" He undid a top button to expose the object more thoroughly. "This is nothing but a sign of old age." He laughed. "It's a ballistic vest—you know, bullet-proof. Supposed to stop anything up to a forty-four Magnum." He relit the cigar. "Cost me forty beans, but I figure it's worth it. I only got three more to go to retirement."

"It must be awfully hot on a night like this," I observed.

"Better hot than embalmed," he said. He rebuttoned his shirt.

Good Lord, another paranoid, I thought as I remembered Sergeant Quinn at the academy. They were all the same way. "Have you patrolled Ninety-five very long?" I asked.

He brushed the cigar on the ashtray and adjusted the radio. "On and off for around seventeen years now," he said.

"Tell me, do you think—"

"Aw, shit!" he exclaimed, lifting the mircrophone. "Two Lima Ninety-five. Go ahead," he said.

"Two Lima Ninety-five . . . report of a man down in the five hundred block of West Main," the dispatcher said. "Ambulance en route."

D'Angelo acknowledged the call and shifted the cigar to the other side of his mouth.

"Someone injured?" I asked. I imagined us racing with siren and emergency lights to the scene of some accident.

"Naw, I doubt it. Probably just a wino. Passed out. Maybe slipped and busted his head on the sidewalk." He turned the cruiser around and drove down a side street. "That isn't even supposed to be our beat," he continued, pointing at the radio. "West Main is Ninety-four's beat. Only there ain't no Ninety-four tonight 'cause we're shorthanded—as usual."

A high-pitched tone sounded from the radio.

"What's that?"

"Emergency call of some kind about to go out," he said. "They always hit that tone first." He turned up the volume.

"Two Lima Ninety-seven," a woman's voice said. "Female subject Singal Zero with potash at Fifteen-seventeen Betton Court, Apartment Six."

I listened as another patrol unit acknowledged the call.

"Now that's on our beat," Angie said, "but they give it to another car since we're already on a call."

"What does that mean, Signal Zero?" I asked.

"It's a code we use for danger to an officer," he said. "Means better watch your ass, you're going in on a bad one. We also use it for a distress call. You know, officer needs assistance—urgent."

We made a left turn and headed down West Main.

"We did away with just about all our other radio codes a couple years back," he said. "I guess the old man thought it made more sense to just talk plain English on the air than all this ten-this, ten-that crap. We still have a few holdovers, though, like Ten-four and Signal Zero. Mostly 'cause they're used so often." He rolled down the window and threw the cigar butt out. "Down in the project every other call is Signal Zero something. Zero with guns. Zero with knives. Zero with pool cues. You'll see."

"Zero with potash?" I said, referring to the radio call we had just heard. "What kind of a situation is that?"

He brushed several flecks of tobacco off his unifrom shirt. "Oh, usually what happens is that a dude has been messing around with some other broad, see? Old lady finds out about it, and she boils herself up a batch of potash on the stove. Then, when he stumbles in drunk in the middle of the night . . . splash! She throws it in his face."

"My God, that's awful!"

"Yeah. You hungry?" he asked.

"Uh, sure."

"Good. Maybe we'll try and grab a bite after this call, before they lay another one on us. I usually try and eat before the animals start coming out. Otherwise you don't get a chance lots of times."

I looked out the window. Cheap movie houses. Pawnshops. Massage parlors. Fleabag hotels. Overflowing trash cans. Skid row.

"There! I knew it," by partner said irritably. "Sonsabitches can't even wait till the rain stops!" He brought the car to a stop just behind the figure of a man lying on the sidewalk. Both the man's feet rested in the gutter as a stream of water coursed over them. "Two Lima Ninety-five, arrival . . . negative on ambulance."

"Suppose he's hurt?" I asked as we got out of the car. We walked over to the prone figure.

"He ain't hurt. Just drunk on his ass," D'Angelo said. He crouched over the man.

"How can you tell? How can you be sure that he isn't a—a diabetic or something?" I said. This could be serious, I thought.

"I can tell," he said as he stood up. "Seventeen years and I can tell, believe me." He looked at me. "Well, Doc, I guess if we're gonna be partners, you gotta start doing some of the work. You handle this one."

"Sure," I said. I bent over the figure on the ground. "Sir, can you hear me?" I shook one of the man's shoulders. Nothing. "Sir, wake up." Still nothing.

I guessed that he must be in his mid-sixties or even seventies from the look of him. He was thin and worn, emaciated looking. The Navy pea jacket he wore was soaking wet from the rain. Several days stubble of beard covered his face.

"Mister . . . mister, wake up now," I said as I shook him harder. I bent closer.

"Lemme 'lone," the figure suddenly growled. It abruptly turned over and bared itself to the rain. I recoiled as the smell of urine and vomit reached my nostrils. A wine bottle which had been nestled between his legs rolled into the gutter with a dull clunk.

The bottoms of my uniform trousers were getting wet. My shoes made squishing sounds as I struggled to sit him up.

"Come on now, old fellow!" I placed both hands under his armpits, held my breath, and pulled.

"Lemme 'lone, goddamn ya!" he said drunkenly. He broke free of my grasp and fell back on the sidewalk, curled into a fetal position, and lay there motionless, still cursing to himself.

A small crowd of people had gathered under the protective cover of a store awning to watch the drama. I looked up at D'Angelo. Beads of water were running off my unifrom cap and dripping down my neck. My mind raced back to the academy for guidance. Drunk calls. Let's see now . . . I thought.

The big policeman stepped forward. "Awright, old timer. Get the hell up!" He grabbed the rubbery figure by both collars of his jacket and jerked him to his feet.

"Hey, leggo! Leggo!" the man protested as his bloodshot eyes rolled vacantly in their sockets.

"Here's your prisoner, Doc."

D'Angelo shoved the drunk toward me. I caught him just as his legs went out from under him. The man clutched at me desperately. I felt the side of the rough face press against mine as I lost my balance and we both rolled onto the sidewalk. My hat fell in the gutter.

"Listen, now, we're trying to help you," I said, retrieving the hat, and putting it back on my head.

"Jesus, Off'cer . . . gimme a break! Give old Alf a break, huh?" he sobbed. He continued to plead and curse as we stumbled toward the patrol car.

I opened the back door.

"Hold it," D'Angelo said. "You're forgetting something. Search him. Nobody goes in the back of my car without getting searched first."

"He's not John Dillinger," I protested. "He's just a drunk."

"No matter. Shake him down," D'Angelo said.

Good Lord! I bent down in front of the man and began going through his pockets. Gloves. Why didn't they issue us gloves for this sort of thing? I wondered as I retrieved a moist rag from one of the man's pockets. It was covered with dried blood and mucus.

"Goddamn whores! Motherfuckers!"

D'Angelo walked up beside me. "That's a great way to search a guy. Great, if you want to get your face kicked in." He snatched the man by the back of his belt and turned him around, palms on the car. Then he kicked the drunk's legs apart with a heavy boot and finished the search himself.

My face flushed. I knew the standard search procedure as well as he did.

"I would have searched him that way if it had been something serious," I said.

"You don't think a drunk can hurt you?" he said as we got into the car. "Listen, you see here?" He pulled back his upper lip and pointed to a space between two teeth. "An old fart about half his size knocked this baby out last year. He damn near put both me and my partner in the hospital. Don't ever kid yourself. A drunk can—"

D'Angelo stopped in midsentence, frowned and sniffed the air. Now I smelled it too. Human feces!

"Goddamn you," D'Angelo shouted. He turned in the seat. "You shit in my car and I'll make you eat it, so help me God!"

The figure on the other side of the wire cage grunted. "Get fucked," it said.

We finished the mercifully short drive to the city jail with the front windows down and the air conditioner on full blast. D'Angelo parked the patrol car in one of the prisoner loading bays behind the jail. "Okay. Now we got to get him up there to the booking area. Give me a hand," he said.

I opened one of the rear doors. The man kicked at my head with both feet as D'Angelo opened the other door and dragged him outside onto the ground. The stench was overpowering.

We went through the booking procedure and then returned to our car.

"You know what they ought to do with guys like that?" D'Angelo said. He got a can of pine-scented deodorant from the glove compartment and began spraying the inside of the car.

"No, what?"

He emerged from the trunk with a jar of rubbing alcohol and some paper towels.

"They ought to put them on an island somewhere. Treat 'em real good. Give 'em any damn thing they want. Then use 'em for parts."

"Parts?"

"Sure. You know, like when some decent person— maybe a little kid—gets sick and needs, say, a lung or a kidney, take it off one of these assholes," he said as he scrubbed the back seat vigorously.

It had stopped raining by the time we checked back in service. The air was clear and fresh. The very streets that had looked unspeakably filthy a short time before now seemed cleansed. Traffic was getting heavy. We eased along in the bumper-to-bumper stream of taillights as the radio crackled. I found myself wondering if we would head for Ninety-five, our own beat, now. I was anxious to see it.

"That there what they issue you?" D'Angelo asked. He gestured toward my nightstick.

"Yes. Why?"

He laughed. "You'll find out why the first time you have to lay it across somebody's head down in the project. Them things ain't worth nothin' in a fight. Get you one of these." He held up a heavy five-cell metal flashlight in one hand.

"You could kill a man if you hit him with something like that," I exclaimed.

"Better him than you," he replied.

He unwrapped a fresh cigar and lit it, tucking the book of matches behind the visor. I noticed a small crucifix pinned to the visor and next to it a curling snapshot of a woman with long black hair and several children.

"Let's eat, huh?" D'Angelo said.

I was just about to reply when I heard our car number on the radio.

"That bitch musta read my mind," he said. "She always waits till I'm starving to mess over me like this." Then, into the mike, "Two Lima Ninety-five, go ahead."

"Two Lima Ninety-five . . . check a report of a stalled truck in the westbound lane of Henessey Boulevard at Fourteenth Street," the woman's voice said.

"Headquarters, be advised that's on Eight-nine's beat," D'Angelo said irritably.

"That is ten-four, Two Lima Ni-yun fi-yuv," the dispatcher replied cooly. "Two Lima Eighty-nine is out of service at General Emergency. No closer unit in service at this time."

"Ten-four," D'Angelo said. "Bitch," he added as he replaced the microphone and changed our direction of travel.

Traffic was still heavy. It took us a full fifteen minutes to snake our way along to the location of the stalled truck.

"I can see it's gonna be a great night," D'Angelo said as we approached the tractor-trailer rig. It was sitting motionless, squarely in the middle of the road, like some giant turtle. Traffic was backed up in both directions as far as I could see. Horns honking. Motorists cursing and shouting at one another.

D'Angelo parked the police car behind the truck and turned on the rotating blue lights on its roof. "Go on over there and see if you can get them cars moving, while I see if I can find out where the hell the driver is," he said.

Good, I thought to myself. This was something I knew I could handle. We had spent quite a bit of time practicing traffic-direction procedures back at the academy. I recalled with satisfaction that I had done fairly well. I walked to the roadway's double yellow line and

surveyed the situation. A man came forward and told
me that the driver of the truck had just parked the rig in
the middle of the street and walked off. I sent him over
to tell D'Angelo while I addressed the traffic problem. I
began giving hand signals to move forward. Gestures to
halt. Something was wrong, I thought to myself. I
stopped and stood there in the street. Only a few people
were paying attention to my directions. Most of the motorists seemed to be ignoring me as they continued to
struggle with one another for access to the only available lane leading around the truck.

"Say, watch what you're doing," I shouted at one
point, as I jumped back just in time to avoid having my
foot run over by a sedan loaded with children and gro-
ceries. What on earth was I doing wrong? Now just
keep calm and think it through, I thought as I stood
there amid the honking horns and the occasional sound
of jamming brakes.

"What the hell you doing out there? Get them cars
moving!" D'Angelo shouted from beside the patrol car,
where he stood calling for a wrecker. The bulky form
began jogging toward me, the keys and equipment on
his belt jangling as he came closer. "Use your whistle,
for Chrissake!"

The whistle. Yes, of course. I clamped it between my
teeth. My mind flashed back to the academy. Was it
one blast for stop and two for go, or two for stop and
one for go?

"No! No! Not that way. You gotta put something
into it. Blow! Like this!" D'Angelo unleashed a pierc-
ing blast from his own whistle and held up both hands.
Traffic screeched to a halt. "These people'll sit here all
night long with their heads up their asses if you let
'em," he said as he smiled incongruously and gestured
for an elderly woman in one lane to move ahead.

D'Angelo spent the next several minutes demonstrat-
ing the finer points of traffic direction to me, occasionally pausing to mutter obscentities under his breath.
("Yeah, *you*, stupid! I mean you! Move it!") Traffic

was moving along fairly well by the time the wrecker arrived.

"I'm starving," my partner said once we had checked back in service. "You like ribs?"

I nodded. He looked like the kind of person with a cast-iron stomach, I thought. We drove several blocks and locked the police car in front of a small diner, walked inside, and made our way to a booth in the back.

A black man behind the counter called out, "Hey, Angie! Where you been, man?"

"Around, Henry. Same old stuff." D'Angelo shook hands with the man and introduced me.

"We don't see you downtown much anymore, Angie," the black man said as he wiped his hands on a cook's apron and smiled, revealing several gold teeth. The two men talked for a minute or so as D'Angelo ordered us each a plate of barbecued pork ribs and large Cokes.

"Henry there is good people," he said after the black man walked away to prepare our order. "He used to own a little shop down by the project, but he finally give it up and moved here. Jitterbugs was all the time breaking in. Robbing the place." He stuck a toothpick between two teeth. "It's the decent colored like Henry I feel sorry for."

I watched the cook unwrap several pieces of meat and drop them on the stove's surface. The delicious smell quickly filled the restaurant. "Do you think most black people are like him?" I asked. Now was probably as good a time as any to start asking questions, I thought.

"Yeah, I think so," he said.

The reply surprised me.

"The problem is that if you're a cop you mostly just see niggers—not colored people like Henry."

A few minutes later the cook brought a steaming platter of ribs and placed it in front of us. D'Angelo continued talking as he gnawed on one of them.

"I'll tell you something," he said. "To me an asshole's just an asshole. It don't make no difference what color he is. If a guy's black or yellow or green and he acts like a man, then I treat him like a man. If he acts like a nigger, he gets treated like a nigger." He wiped his mouth with a paper napkin and picked up another rib. "Same way with whites and honkies. Don't make no difference." He adjusted the volume on the portable radio between us. "It's easy for a cop to get where he hates anybody who's colored, some of the shit that happens to you."

He shook his head and gulped the Coke.

"Like you take last week for instance. Me and my partner get an OD call—drug overdose—down in the project. We go inside this filthy goddamn hole and there's a kid, maybe sixteen—seventeen, on the floor, about gone. Just barely breathing and all. His folks and everybody else are just standing around, not doing a goddamn thing." He discarded the second rib and picked up another, licking the sweet red sauce from his fingers. "Anyway, I start giving the kid mouth-to-mouth. Not that I like kissing colored, but it's either that or the kid dies. That's my job, right? So I keep it up until the ambulance guys get there. The kid makes it okay, and I feel pretty good about the whole thing." A belch. "Then next day I go into the hospital to get a statement from him and what does he give me? Fuck you, pig! All that kinda shit!"

"Maybe he didn't realize what you'd done," I volunteered.

"The hell he didn't!" D'Angelo said. He pointed a rib bone at me across the table. "I heard the nurse tell him, 'That policeman who pulled you through last night wants to talk to you.'"

I was about to say something when the emergency tone sounded from our portable radio. "Headquarters to Two Lima Ninety-five and Two Lima Ninety-seven."

D'Angelo acknowledged the call through a mouthful of meat as he stood up. He fished a dollar bill from his pocket without waiting for the dispatcher to continue her transmission. I did likewise.

Another emergency tone, followed by the female voice again. Her speech was hurried, edged wtih tension. "All units stand by . . . emergency radio traffic only."

D'Angelo glowered at the radio in his palm. "C'mon . . . put it out!"

"Two Lima Ninety-five, Two Lima Ninety-seven . . . robbery in progress."

My pulse jumped.

"Silent hold-up alarm at Eighteenth and Chipley . . . Speedy Rent-a-Car," the voice said.

"Ninety-five rolling from Third and Main," D'Angelo said. He bolted toward the front door and I followed him. The black-and-white car started with a roar and lurched away from the curb.

My heart was pounding. "How far away are we?" I asked.

"Too damned far," he said. He punched the gas pedal and turned on the emergency lights. It was dark. The bright pinwheels of the blue light reflected off windows and the sides of buildings as we passed. I groped for my seat as I watched the speedometer needle creep steadily forward.

Robbery calls. I tried to remember the instructions and exercises I had been through at the academy. I couldn't seem to think clearly. Couldn't concentrate on anything. Everything was whipping by my window in a dizzying blur. A kaleidoscope of pavement, people, cars.

"Headquarters to all units on the silent at Eighteenth and Chipley . . . be advised that is a valid alarm . . . Suspect is a black male wearing military fatigues and a stocking cap . . . last seen running south on Chipley. Suspect reportedly Signal Zero with a sawed-off shotgun. Stand by for additional description," the dispatcher said.

The last words stuck in my mind. Signal Zero with a shotgun! I looked at the radio and felt my insides tighten. I suddenly wanted to be somewhere else. Anywhere else.

"Move, you piece of shit!" D'Angelo commanded our car. I pressed both feet hard against the floorboard and shoved my back against the seat as we approached the next intersection. Two solid lines of cars blocked our direction of travel. I started to turn the siren control to an ON position. D'Angelo brushed my hand away. He would later explain to me that only television policeman can afford to use a siren on their way to an in-progress robbery or burglary call—for the simple and obvious reason that it serves to warn criminals from a great distance away that the police are coming. I closed my eyes as he swerved over the double line to the obvious terror of several oncoming drivers who hit their brakes.

"He'll be headed back for the project," he said to himself.

We cut around another line of cars and returned to the right side of the road. A police helicopter churned the air noisily as it passed us. And then we were on Chipley Avenue. I reached down and unsnapped the service revolver as I saw the street sign. Moments later D'Angelo sped past another sign, SPEEDY RENT-A-CAR on a plate-glass window, and shot into an alley several blocks beyond it. Cats scattered off garbage cans, and cardboard boxes fell in every direction at our approach. The cruiser bumped and squeaked through rain-filled potholes, splashing mud on the freshly washed white door panels. We emerged at the other end of the alley.

"What are we going to do?" I asked.

D'Angelo gave no sign of having heard me as he glanced up and down the street. "Maybe down to Jefferson. Then up to Washington," he said. "Yeah."

The patrol car made a sharp turn and accelerated again. Twenty minutes later we were still crisscrossing the area with other patrol units in a search for the suspect. D'Angelo relaxed in his seat, offering me half a stick of gum and popping the remainder into his mouth.

"Long gone," he said. "No way we'll catch him now. May as well go on back and get started on our report."

The girl behind the cash register at Speedy Rent-a-Car was still ashen-faced when we walked in. She explained that the man who robbed her was shaking badly and kept telling her that he was sorry about having to do this, but he was sick and needed the money.

"Hype," Angie said simply as he penned in a line in the middle of the robbery report. He turned to me. "He didn't get much. They'd just made a deposit, so he might come back out for another hit later on tonight."

"You think so?" I asked, somehow unable to accept the idea that a person would consider committing such a serious and dangerous crime twice in the same evening.

"Sure," he said as we got back in the patrol car. "It all depends on just how bad he's hurting for a fix. How big a habit he's got. All these cats gotta do is slip back into the project and change clothes. Then you can't tell 'em from anybody else on the streets."

I wasn't listening to him. I was thinking about the robber. The addict. The social, psychological and economic factors behind drug addiction. I understood them well, I thought. Yet even understanding their causation, their etiology, I had still unsnapped the gun, I told myself with a pang of guilt. Why? Suppose we had come upon the shaking addict as he was coming out of the door with the shotgun. What would I have done? Would I have shot him? Was I actually capable of doing a thing like that? I remembered Quinn and the range as a drop of perspiration rolled down one armpit.

The paper man suddenly seemed real for the first time.

5

THE BEAT

I uncapped my fountain pen and began writing.

Friday, 1 June 1973. Finished first night as a patrolman. Can already see that project should afford an excellent opportunity to explore dynamics of the police personality . . .

I put the pen aside for a moment. I must be sure to keep a meticulous diary of everything that happened, I told myself. The log could yield a wealth of data that might be analyzed once I returned to the university. A book perhaps, I thought; a number of original scientific papers.

I continued writing:

Applicability of several tenets of Thornton's theory of police personality dramatically evident in attitudes and behavior of first riding partner. Veteran patrolman. Hyperaggressive tendencies evident. Diffuse hostility. Cynicism.

I paused and looked at the uniform hanging in one corner of my room. All the world's a stage, I thought. Well, I could play this part successfully enough once I got used to it. I finished recording the night's events and went to sleep.

The following evening Ron D'Angelo and I headed directly toward Beat Ninety-five after roll call. We wouldn't have to cover Ninety-four tonight. It had kept us from ever getting to our own beat that first night.

West Allison Street was the heart of the city's black ghetto and the beginning of our beat, D'Angelo explained. He made a turn and rolled down his window. I looked around me as we drove slowly down the street. Black faces. Men, women and children of all ages moving in and out of cramped shops. Small restaurants. Bars. Pool halls. Signs. MATTIE'S PLACE—SOUL FOOD, CONK SALAD SPECIAL TODAY, KNIGHTS OF PYTHIAS LODGE NO. 314, FLOSSIE MAE'S CONFECTIONERY, BLUE BIRD CAFE. The sights and sounds seemed to engulf me. Black voices. Talking. Laughing. Arguing. The smell of a food I couldn't identify. Pool balls colliding with one another. A trace of smoke in the night air. It smelled good, I thought, like the barbecue place the night before.

D'Angelo slowed the cruiser to a crawl and stopped in front of a place called Ace's Tavern. He sat watching several black youths standing in front of it.

"Is anything wrong?" I asked.

"More'n likely," he replied. "Just about everybody in there is into something."

The young males watched us with expressionless faces as he put the car in gear and continued down the block. I studied several examples of graffiti on the walls of passing buildings. "Tony been here," one of the inscriptions' blue letters proclaimed. "Marie suck donkey dick," another one accused in green spray paint. "Kill Whitey," a third said ominously.

"Hey, D'Angelo, baby! What's happening, man?" The voice called at us as we stopped for a traffic light, the words trailed by laughter.

"Get fucked, scumbag," D'Angelo muttered to himself.

I turned and saw the man who had spoken as we drove off. He was leaning against the side of a late-model Cadillac with one arm around an attractive black girl.

"Who was that?" I asked.

"That's Mr. Clean," D'Angelo said. He braked the cruiser to let a toothless old woman with a fruit cart pass in front of us. "He's a pusher. Supplies a lot of the heroin down here." He glanced in his rearview mirror. "Look at that. Ten to one he's dealing dope back there right now." He slowed to wave at a black man who was selling watermelons out of the back of a pickup truck. "I remember when you could lock up an asshole like that just on general principles. Not no more. That's 'harassment.' I stop Mr. Clean back there and shake his tree real good like I should, and I'd be up at Internal Affairs on a complaint first thing in the morning."

I rolled up my window as the smell of a dead cat, its carcass flattened by countless tires, wafted inside the patrol car.

"Better leave that down," he cautioned. "You got to be able to hear things down here."

I rolled the window back down.

"Headquarters to Two Lima Ninety-five . . . "

"I'll get it," I said. I lifted the mike, pleased that I had recognized our car number. I wondered if he had noticed. "Two Lima Ninety-five, go ahead."

"Two Lima Ninety-five . . . see the woman. A larceny complaint at Twenty-two Court Echo, Apartment Five-A."

"Ten-four," I acknowledged. I replaced the microphone and jotted the address on a pad in my lap. "Is that the housing project?" I asked.

D'Angelo nodded.

Good, I thought. I was starting to feel more confident. Working in the ghetto would be no problem. I was used to working with black people, particularly black people in trouble with the law. I had been employed on and off during graduate school as a prison counselor and also a juvenile probation worker at a ranch for delinquent boys. A large segment of my case load on both jobs had been black. I looked up ahead. I could see the dark, high buildings of the Abraham Street Housing Development. The project. D'Angelo drove into it, maneuvering the cruiser around a broken tricycle in the middle of the road. I looked out my window. Only concrete splinters of what had once been street signs remained as a means of differentiating one street from another. Masses of yellow weeds had long since seized absolute control of every yard in sight. Makeshift clotheslines drooped dismally in front of apartment buildings badly in need of repair. Debris dotted the passing landscape: partially dismantled cars and motorcycles, overflowing garbage cans, scattered newspapers, empty food containers, broken pieces of what looked like playground equipment.

"What was that address?" D'Angelo asked.

I shined the flashlight on my notebook. "Twenty-two Court Echo, Apartment Five-A," I said.

We made a turn and started down another street, watched by an old woman who sat rocking and fanning herself on a wooden porch. A beam of light from the cruiser's spotlight soon revealed the apartment number we were looking for.

"Here, Doc," D'Angelo said. "We'll start giving you a little practice with report writing." He tore a white form entitled CRIME AGAINST PROPERTY off a thick pad and handed it to me. I picked up my clipboard and attached the portable radio to my Sam Browne belt as we started walking up a cracked cement walkway leading to one of the apartment buildings. I pulled the torn screen door back and raised my hand to knock.

D'Angelo grabbed my arm and pulled me to one side. "You ain't even gonna make it through your second night if you don't shape up. Don't never stand in front of a door like that. Good way to get yourself blown away." He reached out with the tip of his flashlight and knocked. No response. He knocked again, louder this time.

"Who dat is?" a child's voice demanded imperiously.

"Po-lice," D'Angelo replied. Running feet.

"Mama, it's the po-lice." A few moments more and

the door was opened a crack by a young black woman.

"What can we do for you, ma'am?" D'Angelo said.

"Been ripped off by somebody," she said. She opened the door and stepped back to admit us. Four small children sat tightly clustered in front of a large black-and-white TV in the living room, absorbed in a Frankenstein movie.

"What happened?" I asked once we entered the kitchen. I positioned the report form on my clipboard and recorded the date and time of our arrival.

The woman clasped a frayed red bathrobe in front of her as she spoke. "We been gone all day," she said. "Somebody musta come in while we was out. Took my purse. It was setting there on the table."

"Was the place locked?" I asked.

"Cain't lock the back door," she said. "Lock's busted off. It was that way when we moved in."

The whole apartment reeked of urine and a chemical smell of some kind. I looked around me. A large black roach scurried about on the kitchen drainboard in search of food. Crusty dishes were piled high in the sink. One of them had slid off onto the floor where it lay in broken pieces. A pile of soiled diapers was mounded in one corner.

"Y'all can sit down if you want," the woman offered. She sank into a chair.

"No thank you, ma'am," I replied, ashamed to realize why I didn't want to sit down. The place was too dirty.

"What'd they get? What was in the purse?" D'Angelo asked.

She lit a cigarette and inhaled deeply. "I had a twenty-dollar bill. Little change." A sigh of resignation. "That's all we had to last till the first," she said.

A little girl with chocolate brown skin appeared in the doorway. Stark naked, dripping water. The child smiled at us.

"Ellie, you get back in there or you gonna get a good whipping," the woman said.

The child scampered back down the hall.

"Are they all yours?" I asked.

She nodded. She couldn't be twenty, I thought. We finished taking the necessary information for our report and got ready to leave. I suggested she have the lock repaired, sensing somehow that it would remain broken. We walked back into the living room just as Frankenstein's monster was dispatching another victim.

"Hey, po-lice!" a little boy of about six shouted. He aimed a broken yardstick at my partner. "Bam! Bam! Bam!"

"Got me!" D'Angelo laughed. He walked over and crouched beside the boy. "What's your name, hotshot?"

"Sammy. Sammy Arnold," he said. "What's your name, po-lice?"

"D'Angelo. People just call me Angie, Sammy."

"Danjello? Dat's a funny name."

"No funnier'n Sammy," he said. He stood and ran a hand across the Brillo-like surface of the boy's head.

"You got a real gun! You shoot lots of people?" the child asked excitedly. His eyes fastened on D'Angelo's holster.

A look came across D'Angelo's face, a certain sadness in the eyes. "I don't like to shoot people, Sammy," he said.

"Then why you got a gun?" the boy piped.

D'Angelo smiled, bent back down. "To protect folks," he said. "Like if somebody tried to hurt you or your mama real bad, I might have to shoot 'em. But I'd try not to. Po-lice don't like to hurt anybody, Sammy."

"Yeah? A po-liceman hit my uncle with a slapjack once, right up side the head," he said. "I seen it. Whop!" The boy slapped a palm against the side of his face.

I thought of my own family, my own childhood. How could a boy that age know about things like slapjacks?

Sammy followed us to the door and waved good-bye. We walked back to the patrol car and got inside.

"What was that smell in there, Angie?"

"The piss or the other?" he asked as he started the car.

"The other."

"That's kerosene, Doc. They use it all over the project as a whaddyacallit—a disinfectant. See, the toilets in these places don't work half the time. So they keep pots with kerosene around to shit and piss in. The kerosene cuts the smell."

"That's awful," I said. "My God, can't the health department do anything?"

He shook his head. "I filed plenty of complaints on these places myself, but it don't do no good. Most of the private landlords live out of town. Health people can't even find 'em a lot of the time."

Nobody should have to use a can filled with kerosene, I told myself. Not today. Not in this country.

The emergency tone. "Headquarters to Two Lima Ninety-one," the radio said. "A shooting at the J and B Club . . . Fifteen-forty-five West Allison. Ambulance en route." Another unit acknowledge the call.

"West Allison? It's on our beat, isn't it?" I said.

"Yeah, only we can't check back in service until we finish this report. That's why they give it to Ninety-one."

I felt secretly relieved that we hadn't received the assignment. We drove several blocks and parked beside a vacant field strewn with beer cans and wine bottles.

An officer's voice came on the air a few minutes later, just as we were finishing the report. "Two Lima Ninety-one to Headquarters," it said. "Better get homicide over here on Allison."

D'Angelo turned to me. "You ever seen a dead body?"

I shook my head.

"We'll take a run on by and see what they've got," he said.

A few minutes later we approached the J and B Club on West Allison. A number of other police units were parked in front of it as we pulled up, their radios blaring in the night. We worked our way through the crowd of people outside and entered the bar just as a flashbulb exploded. When my eyes recovered, I saw a form sprawled on the floor next to an overturned chair across the room.

"You know him, Angie?"

"Leroy!" D'Angelo exclaimed with feigned anguish. He walked over and stood beside the body.

"You know him, Angie?" asked a man with a loosened tie and shoulder holster.

"Did I know him? Leroy Owens was my prize A-number-one pimp," he said. "And you guys let him get killed! What the hell kinda police force we got in this city when a decent pimp like Leroy here can't walk the streets without getting knocked off, huh?"

The other men in the room laughed. I shuddered, wondering how they could possibly see anything funny.

The evidence techincians moved methodically about the bar, occasionally stepping over or around the body as they examined and paced the area. Another flashbulb popped. I stood at the opposite end of the bar, carefully averting my eyes from the corpse, hoping we would leave soon.

"Hey, buddy," the man with the camera called out to me. He motioned me over to him. "Give me a hand, will you?"

I swallowed hard and started across the room on unsteady feet. It's just a dead body, nothing to be frightened of, I assured myself.

"Hold this flashlight here. Nice and steady." He pointed to an empty shell casing beside the body, handed me the light, and stepped back with his camera. I took it and crouched next to the corpse.

"Just a little more to the left. There, that's it!"

I felt sick at my stomach, light-headed. For a moment I thought I was going to pass out. A flash. Another one.

"Just one more quickie," the photographer said.

I looked at the dead man for the first time. He was a black man in his mid-twenties. His mouth was slightly open in a look of surprise and he still smelled of cologne or after-shave lotion. The eyes were glassy. I saw the small dark hole in the center of his broad nose. Co-

agulated blood covered the paisley shirt he wore,
stained the bar's light wooden floor well beyond the
white chalk line someone had drawn around the body.
A wide-brimmed felt hat lay on the floor directly behind and to the left of his head. So this was what it
looked like, I thought. Violent death. So still. So much
blood from such a small wound. I stood and handed the
cameraman back his flashlight. How many people had I
seen shot to death on television shows and in movies
over the years? I wondered. It had never looked anything like this before. I felt a chill and stepped back
from the body.

D'Angelo bent down and shined his flashlight on the
dead man's face. "Twenty-five automatic," he said.
"That's a nasty little gun. Twenty-five's, twenty-two's,
and thirty-two's—you stay down here for twenty years
and you won't see many bigger guns. Don't ask me why.
I guess it's the dough. Little guns are so cheap." He
stood up. "I'd almost sooner get hit with a thirty-eight.
There's something about those little guns. They shoot a
guy maybe just once with one and chances are he's
gonna kick off. Ain't that right, Charlie?"

The photographer grunted assent as he readied himself for another shot.

D'Angelo turned to another uniformed man in the
bar. "Hey, Ed, you remember that one we had over on
Norton last week?"

The man nodded and D'Angelo turned back to me.
"This guy gets shot once in the shoulder by a broad he's
shacking with, see?" he said. "Just a little old piddly
twenty-two short! And this is a great big sonofabitch.
Arms as big around as your legs. When we get there,
he's flexing his muscles and all. Says he ain't even hurt.
Wouldn't even let us call an ambulance. Walks into the
emergency room under his own steam. Well, brother,
forty-five minutes later that sucker's stone dead."

"Headquarters to Two Lima Ninety-five . . ." The
radio on my belt. Good, I thought, a call. Anything to
get away from the J and B Club.

"Two Lima Ninety-five . . . take a domestic disturbance at sixteen-nineteen Court India," the dispatcher said.

D'Angelo hesitated at the door as we started to leave. He tipped his hat as he looked back at the body. "*Adios,* MF!"

How could any job make a man that callous? I wondered as we got back inside the car. I found it hard to believe that the man next to me was the same person who had been so gentle with the child back in the project. I would discover in time that callousness becomes a tool in a policeman's life, one that he learns to use in order to keep himself from being engulfed by the horror and trauma around him, to keep himself from succumbing to the madness of other men.

"Aw, no. . . ."

I looked over at D'Angelo as he pulled to the curb. "What's the matter?"

"Air conditioning's out again," he said. "I swear to Christ, this cheap city . . . !" He got a toolbox out of the trunk and spent the next several minutes under the hood, pounding. And cursing. "When they first come out with this take-home-patrol-car plan, all us guys figured it'd be a real good deal," he went on once he was back inside the car. "I mean being able to use the cruiser with free gas off duty sounded pretty nice. It was supposed to work out to around a twelve-hundred-buck-a-year raise for each of us."

"That does sound good," I said.

"Good, my ass!" he snorted. "Good for the city! Now they got us working our butts off twenty-four hours a day, three hundred sixty-five days a year for damn near free." He offered me another stick of gum, which I declined. "There ain't no way to escape being a cop when you're driving a black-and-white every place you go. I'll give you a good example. Monday and Tuesday are my regular days off. Monday's really the only chance I ever really get to sleep late 'cause I got a security job working in a store downtown the rest of the week. The extra bucks come in handy, you know?

"Anyway, last Monday the whole family is sound

asleep when this clown from out of town pulls up. He spots the black-and-white parked in my driveway. 'Oh, a policeman,' he says to himself. Five o'clock in the morning, now! Five o'fucking clock in the morning!" He shook one hand in front of his face. "This jerk starts beating on my door like he was the Gestapo or something. Says he wants to know where the Lindmar Expressway is!" He clenched his teeth. "I come close to punching his eyes out."

As he spoke, an ancient tan car pulled out in front of us, its single exhaust pipe belching clouds of black smoke. D'Angelo turned on the blue lights. "If there's anything I can't stand, it's somebody fouling up the air I got to breathe!" He picked up the mike as the car eased over to the curb and stopped. "Two Lima Ninety-five to Headquarters . . . be out on a vehicle stop in the four thousand block of Jefferson. Light brown fifty-five Chevy. License plate AKT-eight-sixty-seven. Alpha Kilo Tango eight-sixty-seven." He got out of the patrol car with his flashlight and citation book.

It was cool now. Pleasant. I relaxed in the seat as I watched D'Angelo begin writing a citation beside the Chevrolet. A short, middle-aged black man stood next to him with his arms folded. I closed my eyes and rubbed them, listening to the steady hum from the police car's rotating emergency lights. I remembered an article I had read recently on the psychology of automobile stops. It had said that there is no greater source of ill will between the police and the public than the routine traffic encounter, and that this is so because it involves placing an adult momentarily in the status of a child—stopping him, controlling him in front of the eyes of others. I opened my eyes as I heard the door of the black-and-white open.

"Where the hell were you?" D'Angelo snapped.

"What do you mean?"

"Why weren't you back there covering me?" he said. "Didn't you learn nothing about car stops at the academy?"

"Of course I did, but this was just an ordinary—"

"Listen, my friend, there ain't no such thing as 'ordinary' down here. Remember that!" He paper-clipped several copies of the citation together and threw them on the dash. The tan Chevolet pulled away. "Suppose that guy up there had just knocked over a store, huh? Suppose he had a gun, maybe somebody hiding in the back seat? He could have wasted me while you were sitting back here with your head up your ass!"

There were several minutes of silence. "All right, I'm sorry," I said cooly, at last. "It won't happen again." It was ridiculous to make such an issue out of something so minor, I thought. Paranoia, I reminded myself. A characteristic of the police personality.

"Look, let's get a few things straight between us, okay?" D'Angelo said.

"Okay."

"I don't really understand why you come out here in the first place and I don't care," he said. "I figure that's your business. But as long as you're sitting over there wearing that shield you're my partner." We turned into the Abraham Street project. "We got to depend on each other," he continued, "especially on a beat like this. Look, it don't matter none to me how much education you got. Some guys don't like to ride with college boys. Me, I don't care one way or the other. I judge a guy by what he does. That's all that matters to me out here. You start off in my book with a clean slate, just like any other rookie. Agreed?"

"Agreed."

"There, that must be it up ahead," he said as he radioed our arrival. We pulled to the curb in front of an apartment building.

"Bobby, you nothing but a jive-assed nigger," a woman shouted.

I watched her as she backed a shirtless black man slowly down the sidewalk toward the curb. She held a long stick in both hands.

"You the nigger, bitch!" he shouted back, retreating a little faster.

"Awright, knock it off!" D'Angelo called out. We

got out of the car. "Doc, go talk to the guy while I get that stick away from her," he instructed.

I started up the walk toward the man.

"C'mon, now, give me that thing. Let's not have no trouble, huh?" D'Angelo said casually.

The woman hesitated, then reluctantly handed him the stick.

I saw several small children standing on the front porch watching the dispute. A number of neighbors had come out of the surrounding apartment units. "Hi, there. What seems to be the trouble?" I said as I walked up to the man. Marital counseling, I thought, remembering how I had once run a prison counseling group for inmates and their wives. A good group, I recalled.

The man in front of me scowled. "Ain't no call for you to be coming round here bothering us," he said. His face contorted as he stared at me. He smelled strongly of liquor.

I smiled and took off my hat, one of the practiced rapport-winning smiles from my days as a correctional worker. The dark chest heaved from deep breaths. "We're not here to cause you any trouble," I said as I touched his shoulder in a reassuring gesture.

"Get your mother-fucking hands off me!" He brushed my arm roughly away.

Something wrong! I tried another one of the techniques I had used in prison and probation work to calm excitable people. "Just relax now! There's nothing to be upset about. All we—"

"You stop telling your lies! Hear me, bitch?" he shouted.

The woman was now standing with a small child in her arms, talking excitedly to D'Angelo. The shirtless man cursed and started toward her.

I stepped in front of him. "Please, just listen to me for a—" I felt a stinging sensation on the side of my face. Then a hand grabbed the front of my unifrom shirt roughly. I stumbled backward, reflexively grabbing the man as I fell. This wasn't happening. It couldn't be, I thought, as we rolled on the ground. Shouts. D'Angelo's voice coming toward me. Fear. For the first time in my life, genuine panic. It broke across me like a giant wave. I groped for my nightstick, realizing as I felt the empty ring that I had left it in the car. Cursing. Grunting. The shirtless figure tore the expansion band on my wristwatch loose, popped a button off one of my shoulder epaulets. I managed to get the handcuffs out of their leather case. Short of breath. I tried to turn the man over. Couldn't. His arms were flailing at me like a windmill.

Then I heard D'Angelo, saw him out of the corner of one eyes. A blue cloud descending on us. Cursing. Breathing heavily from running. He snatched the man away from me and flipped him easily over onto his back in the weeds. "C'mon! Hurry up!" he said. He wrenched his arms together. I rasped the handcuff teeth in place. We stood there for a moment trying to catch our breath.

"What the hell did you say to the guy?"

"I—"

"Don't hurt my man! Don't hurt him!"

I turned just in time to see the woman. She was charging toward us with a raised stick, the stick D'Angelo had just taken away from her.

"Ow! Gimme that goddamn thing!" my partner said as she delivered a blow to the arm he had raised in front of his face. He grabbed her wrist and squeezed until she howled in pain and dropped the stick. The children on the porch were crying now.

"Mama, mama," one of the smaller boys said as he jumped off the porch and ran toward us. "Don't you hurt my mama! Don't hurt her!" he sobbed, as he began pounding ineffectually on one of the big policeman's legs.

D'Angelo looked at the boy for a long moment, then released his grip on the woman. "I oughta book you. You know that?" he said angrily as he glared at her. He massaged his arm and looked back at the child, who now stood clinging to her dress. "I probably would, too, except I don't wanta go to all the trouble of putting these kids in the shelter tonight."

I looked at the boy and saw the look of hatred and fear etched on his small features as he watched us. My God, what had we done to earn the hatred of a child? I wondered.

We started toward the car with our prisoner, dragging him because he refused to walk. I panted as we moved the mass of dead weight slowly across the yard. Passive resistance, I thought, as my mind went back to Berkeley and the sit-in demonstrations I had seen. I grunted as I pulled one of the warm brown arms and remembered the sight of students being dragged off and loaded into police vans. Long hair. Beards. Girls in jeans flashing occasional V signs at news cameramen. The cause, I thought. Just what had the cause really been? Vietnam? Free Speech? Civil Rights? It had never been altogether clear to me, lost, perhaps, somewhere in all the rhetoric and turmoil of protest. "Off the pigs! Off the pigs!" I remembered the chanting voices from Sproul Plaza.

I looked back as we reached the car and saw the woman disappear inside with her children, and I wondered why the little boy had seemed so worried about her yet so unconcerned about the handcuffed figure whom I took to be his father. In time I would learn the answer to that question, would discover that women, along with poverty, were perhaps the only completely dependable feature of a ghetto child's existence. Men came and went. Bred children. Got drunk. Spent the welfare money on liquor and gambling. Committed crimes. Got caught by The Man and went to jail— prison from time to time. Became part of the endless cycle of in and out. Only women endured as beacons of stability here in the ghetto. Only they might truly be counted on, depended upon. Mothers. Grandmothers. Aunts. Sisters. Daughters.

"I'll go around and drag him through," D'Angelo said.

I stood there beside the door, looking at the prisoner, feeling a vague sense of remorse over what had happened, a strange sort of culpability. I had just used force against another human being for the first time in my life. I stepped closer and leaned over the back seat. "Why—"

A blinding white flash of pain hit me as the man swung one bare foot off the seat and struck me squarely in the genitals. I staggered backward and dropped to my knees.

"You sonofabitch!" D'Angelo shouted. He jerked the back door on his side open and brought one hand down hard across the man's face.

Something incredibly primitive seized control of me, a consuming desire to attack, to utterly destroy. I knelt there in the weeds, wishing that I had the nightstick, conscious of a desire to bludgeon the man with it.

D'Angelo ran over and helped me to my feet. "You okay, Doc?" he asked.

I nodded, gasping as we reached the patrol car. I clung to one of the cruiser's doorposts for support and brought my face close to the wire cage. "I'm charging you with resisting arrest with violence. Do you understand that?" I shouted.

"Shee-it!" The man laughed. A rivulet of bright red blood trickled down from one of his nostrils. In time, I would grasp the simple truth that you can take nothing from a man who has nothing.

As we drove toward the jail with our prisoner, I thought how very different the situation I had just been through was from anything I had ever experienced as a correctional worker. Counselors, psychiatrists and social workers—unlike policemen—are rarely subject to physical attack by the people they are trying to help. I had never before had to face another human being as a patrolman must learn to: when the person is at his worst—violent, hysterical, desperate. The day I put the blue uniform on, I lost the luxury of dealing with interpersonal problems under calm and carefully controlled circumstances.

An hour passed before we finished booking the man

and returned to patrol. I was still bruised and sore, but starting to feel a little better.

"You wanta run by the emergency room and have 'em take a look at you?" D'Angelo said.

"No. I'll be all right, thanks," I said.

Violence, I thought. The ultimate confession of inarticulateness. What had happened to me back there? I wondered. Fighting with another man like some kind of animal. That wasn't me. I tried to reconstruct the incident in my mind, step by step. Methodically. Logically.

"Hey, you done okay back there, Doc," D'Angelo said. The cruiser's interior filled with smoke from one of his cigars. "Not that you're a born brawler, mind you, but you done okay. You got balls. I'll give you that."

"I'm not so sure anymore," I said.

He laughed. "A word of advice," he said. "Don't never leave yourself wide open like that. One of those bastards'll kill you if you give him half a chance."

We rode along in the darkness, drifting up and down the project streets. The poverty was appalling. Seeing it, smelling it, was so different from reading about it, lecturing about it. Trite but true, I thought.

"Can't they do anything about the conditions down here?" I asked.

D'Angelo shook his head gravely. "Doc, it wouldn't do any good if they rebuilt the whole thing tomorrow," he said. "It'd be right back where it is now inside a month. See them cans over there?" He pointed to a number of garbage cans that had been tipped over into the street.

"Yes."

"A couple years back they decided they was really going to clean up the project," he said, "so they went around sticking up all them 'Don't Be a Litterbug' signs everywhere. Then they started putting great big green trash dumpsters on every corner. You know, in place of the garbage cans."

"What happened?" I asked.

"What happened," he said, "was that the niggers

started setting fires in the dumpsters. Got so it happened about every night." He slowed the cruiser for a moment to jot down the license plate number on an out-of-state car. "And when the fire trucks would roll up, the nigger'd snipe at 'em. It got to be a game. Niggers setting fires. Fire guys coming in, getting shot at, niggers setting more fires, us tied up escorting fire units all night long." He threw his cigar out the window. "Anyway, they finally give up and pulled out all the dumpsters. Now it's back the way it was again."

The rest of the night was mercifully slow, marked only by a succession of minor complaint calls. A barking dog. A landlord-tenant dispute. A false alarm at a men's clothing store. D'Angelo declared that we had been lucky for a Saturday night. " 'Night, Doc. See you tomorrow," he said after we checked off duty at the station.

"Tomorrow," I echoed unthinkingly.

I drove back to the Raleigh and wearily climbed the stairs. Brooding. Depressed. I sat at my kitchen table, staring at the logbook. Finally I began writing.

Saturday, 2 June 1973. Second night as a patrolman. Worked Beat No. 95 for the first time tonight. Involved in a fight. Hard to explain how it all started, really. A domestic situation that got out of hand somehow, escalated. Unavoidable, I think . . .

I went back and crossed out the word "fight." It was really a misnomer. I replaced it with "scuffle." In the months ahead I would find that that is largely what a policeman does when he is said to have been in a fight. He rarely, if ever, "fights" anyone, at least not in the John Wayne sense of the word: standing toe to toe, exchanging a series of neck-breaking, roundhouse blows with another man. In situations where a policeman must truly fight, nature's tool is pathetically feeble— television stereotypes aside—when compared to the damage that can be wrought by a well-placed nightstick or a five-cell flashlight. Mostly, a street officer becomes as adept as he can at the business of scuffling with other people. He grunts, kicks, hangs on, grabs hold of anything he can—tries desperately to end the struggle before he runs out of breath. Quickly, because he realized the unique danger he is in whenever he scuffles with another person. There is always a gun present.

I finished the log and slipped into bed. Tomorrow night would be better, I promised myself as I switched off the light.

6

PARTNERS

WE moved along West Main Street with the evening flow of traffic. The watch was shorthanded again and we were covering both Ninety-four and Ninety-five until extra cars came on duty at ten o'clock. Even though it was not yet dark, many of the topless bars and movie theaters we passed already had their multicolored lights glowing brightly.

"Your family?" I asked. I pointed at the snapshot over D'Angelo's visor.

"That's most of it." He smiled. "I got two other kids that ain't in this picture. You got kids, Doc?"

"A boy ten and a baby on the way," I said. I took a picture of Merry Ann and Craig out of my wallet and showed it to him.

"How's your old lady feel about you being a cop?" he asked.

But I'm not a cop, Angie, I thought to myself. I'm a scientist who just happens to be wearing a police uniform. I'm out here to study you. "She's not very keen about the idea," I replied.

He laughed. "They're all alike. Mine's the same way. Even after all these years, she's still on me to quit and get a regular job. She don't like me being a cop." He reached in his shirt pocket and removed a photograph laminated in plastic. "That's my baby, Linda," he said as he handed it to me. A pretty girl in her late teens with dark eyes and long black hair. "She's going to college up north. Engaged to a guy already. It really makes me feel old."

Was this what policemen did? I wondered. Drive along talking about their wives and children like other men? I was about to say something when I heard the emergency tone, followed by our car number.

"Two Lima Ninety-five . . . a suicide attempt in progress at Sixteen-fifteen Blainey. Amublance is en route," the dispatcher said.

D'Angelo accelerated and motioned for me to turn on the emergency lights and siren. This was the way things usually happened, I would find. Suddenly. With no warning. Right in the middle of a sentence, a mouthful of food, a cup of coffee, at the most illogical, inconvenient times. A surge of adrenaline punctuating minutes of relative calm. Man down! Robbery in progress! Major injury accident! Domestic disturbance! See the woman! And almost always the calls would come without the precious luxury of time. Time. I had come to take it for granted in my life as a university professor. Time to think situations through, time to analyze them, dissect them. Time to weigh the desirability of different courses of action.

The siren's yelp echoed off the sides of passing buildings and filled the black-and-white's interior, all but drowning out the dispatcher's voice.

"Two Lima Ninety-five arrival," I said as we pulled to the curb several blocks later. A number of people were gathered on the lawn in front of a brown stucco apartment building.

"He's up there in Number Eight!" a bald man said excitedly as he ran up to my window. He thrust a wrinkled pice of paper at me through the window:

Nothing left. Can't go on. Tell Carla I'm sorry.

"Me and my wife were just getting ready to go out to a movie when we saw the note," he continued.

I could hear the distance wail of another siren as we got out and ran toward the staircase.

D'Angelo said nothing as he bounded up the steps

two at a time with me behind him. "Police! Open up in there!" he shouted as he beat on the door of Apartment Eight. Nothing. He beat again. Still nothing. People were standing around on the landing, watching us, whispering to one another. An ambulance braked at the curb down below.

"What are we going to do?" I asked. We should call for a sergeant, I thought. I was trying to remember something from the academy about the legality of forced entry into private dwellings.

"Stand back!" D'Angelo said as he raised one foot and brought it down hard against the door. Another kick. Another. The ambulance men were starting up the stairs with a stretcher. D'Angelo kicked once more and the door sprung open.

I stepped back for an instant. The smell of gas inside the littered apartment was overpowering. Then I saw the man: a white man, lying in one corner of the kitchen, clad only in a pair of jockey shorts. His head was propped inside an open oven and there was a rubber tourniquet knotted around his neck. I tried to hold my breath as I helped D'Angelo drag the limp figure across the living-room rug. I was sure he was dead. I struggled with a flaccid arm. The eyes were closed. The tongue rolled easily in one corner of a discolored mouth. Dead, like the man at the J and B Club, I thought, with a mounting sense of horror. I gulped the fresh air outside on the landing. D'Angelo pulled a small switchblade knife from one boot and cut the tourniquet as I felt the man's wrist frantically for a pulse. The ambulance crew began administering oxygen. Soon the man was coughing and wheezing.

D'Angelo looked down and shook his head. "You dumb sonofabitch," he said as he wiped his forehead, "you almost made it."

The crowd began drifting off as we reached the bottom of the stairs and helped the white-uniformed attendants load the stretcher into the back of the ambulance. It pulled away as the last of the spectators walked off. Wait a minute, I thought. We'd just saved a man's life.

Wasn't someone—anyone—going to say something? It seemed as if someone should say something to us.

"Better answer it, Doc," D'Angelo said.

"What?"

He pointed to the portable radio on my belt.

"Headquarters to Two Lima Ninety-five . . . do you copy?" a female voice said.

I acknowledged.

"Two Lima Ninety-five, we're holding a wreck at Mariposa and Fifth when you're back in service. No closer available unit at this time," she said.

"Ten-four," I said. I sensed the edge in my voice. Another call? Didn't she know what we'd been doing?

"Let's wind this one up for right now, Doc," D'Angelo said. "We can run by the hospital later and get what we need for our report. We better get on over to Mariposa and clear up that wreck before they have another one."

I was thinking about the man who had had his head in the oven. I had never saved anyone's life before. I felt good about it, wanted to talk about it. I started to say something to Angie, but I noticed that he was already pulling out the forms we would need to work the traffic accident.

It was a minor accident. I stood beside our cruiser writing one of the motorists a citation for following too closely.

"You know something?" the man said. "If you guys would spend a little more time worrying about crime and a little less trying to make your ticket quotas, this city might be a decent place to live."

I looked at him. A middle-aged man in a gray business suit. I said nothing. I pressed the pen harder against the ticket book and continued writing as D'Angelo directed traffic.

"No wonder people don't respect the police," the motorist said. He snatched the citation I held out to him out of my hand.

"Yessir," I said. Who the hell does this jerk think he's talking to? I said to myself. Then I thought, To a man in a police uniform, that's who, as I answered my own question. I wasn't used to being talked down to like some kind of lackey. I didn't like it.

We finished clearing the wreck and returned to patrolling the downtown area around West Main. It was teeming with people now. I looked out my window and studied the passing signs. NUDORAMA—ALL-STAR CAST! promised a sign in front of a place called the Kitten Klub. Above it, a large pink neon cat with superimposed human mammaries winked an invitation. NO COVER! WHAT YOU SEE IS WHAT YOU GET, a sign outside another place assured passersby. ALL BOY REVUE, proclaimed a third in an obvious appeal to a more select audience.

D'Angelo pulled to the curb. "We'll get out and walk the strip for a while," he said.

I started to get out and hesitated. I reached back inside, got the nightstick and slipped it in my ring.

"We'll lock the car up down here, but never when we're on Allison or around the project," D'Angelo said. "Remember that."

"Why's that?" I asked as we started walking along the sidewalk.

" 'Cause I don't want to have to waste time busting a window if we need that shotgun in a hurry down there some night. I'd sooner let 'em steal everything in the car," he said. "It all belongs to the city anyway."

We paused in front of a place called The Candle Book and Novelty Shop, and I followed him inside. The proprietor of the store, a diminutive man with pencil-thin arms and eyes that seemed to blink involuntarily, looked up from the newspaper he was reading. I had once spent several weeks as a graduate student at Berkeley researching the subject of pornography for a term paper, but I had really never seen anything quite like The Candle: rack upon rack of magazines and paperbacks, their bright covers portraying in graphic detail for connoisseurs of pornography a limitless variety of sexual acts and actors. We passed a counter covered with an assortment of sexual appliances. Artificial vaginas. Rubber penises of different sizes and colors.

D'Angelo took one of the magazines from a rack and began leafing through it. Something irreverently entitled *The Twat-Licker's Bible*. He turned and looked at the little man behind the counter as he spoke in a loud voice. "I remember when we used to lock people up for having trash like this."

Several people in the store watched as the manager put his paper down and walked over to us. "See here, Officer! You've got no right—"

"Doc, when I worked day watch down here, I used to come in and find little kids—junior high kids—reading this shit," D'Angelo interrupted.

"I'm not violating any law. You can't—"

"Yeah? Where's your business permit?" D'Angelo said.

A well-dressed man exited quickly from the store, followed by two other people.

"I've got it right over there behind the counter," the manager snapped.

D'Angelo smiled. "The law says it's supposed to be posted in plain view, friend," he said. He took a municipal citation book out of his back pocket.

"You're trying to ruin my business," the little man shouted.

D'Angelo looked up from the citation he had begun writing. "Now why would I do a thing like that?" he said. He finished writing the ticket and handed it to the man.

"This isn't the end of this. I'm going to file a complaint! I want your badge number."

"It's on the citation, asshole," D'Angelo said casually as we walked toward the door. He paused outside the shop and looked back inside as he lit a cigar. "You know what I'd like to do, Doc? I'd like to get me a flame thrower and sneak back down here real late some night. Then *whooosh!*" he said as he immolated The Candle and its manager in an imaginary inferno.

Next we walked inside a topless bar and stood for

several minutes watching a girl with striking red hair and small breasts as she undulated atop a platform. She stared vacantly around the room, dancing zombielike amid the smoke and laughter.

"Broads like that are trouble, Doc," D'Angelo said. "Half of 'em are hookers and the other half fuck scumbags and thugs. We just busted a dame in that place we come out of that was driving a getaway car at robberies," he said.

We walked back down the street and got in our car.

"Take it from me, there's nothing in the world that'll get a cop in trouble faster than a broad," he said. We pulled into traffic. "I got to fooling around with a topless dancer a few years back," he went on. "A twenty-five-year-old kid. Me old enough to be her father. I shoulda had my head examined. Guys are idiots when it comes to broads, you know? I went with her pretty regular for a while. Even had a key to her apartment. Anyway, one night I come up to her place unexpected like and there she is sitting on a pillow in the middle of the floor—with a spike in her arm, shooting up!"

"What did you do?" I asked.

He shrugged his shoulders. "What the hell could I do?" he said. "I just dropped the key on the floor and walked out. I never went back. I hear she's a righteous junkie now. Whoring and all. Too bad. I liked her."

We stopped by the hospital and picked up the additional information we needed to finish our report on the attempted suicide. Then dinner in a Chinese restaurant, where D'Angelo ate mountains of rice and egg foo yung soaked in soy sauce.

"Eight-thirteen to Two Lima Ninety-five," the radio said as we got back inside the car after dinner.

D'Angelo sighed, belched. "Don't answer it," he said. "Maybe he'll go away."

"Eight-thirteen to Two Lima Ninety-five," the man's voice repeated. "Do you copy?"

D'Angelo took the microphone from me and acknowledged.

"Meet me at Allison and Lee in five sharp," the voice said.

"Who was that?" I asked as we drove off.

"That was Douche. You ain't met him yet 'cause he's been on vacation."

"Who?"

"Our fearless squad leader, Sergeant Roger T. Bernard, the Second—better known to those of us who love and serve him as just plain Douche. Christ, if he's the Second, I'd sure as hell hate to see the First," he added sarcastically.

"I gather you don't like him much," I said.

"Oh, it's not me," he said. "It's the brass downtown that must hate him. I figure they must be trying to get him killed and they know this is the best place in the city to do it. That's why they transferred him to A Squad. They know that if the niggers don't kill him, one of us guys will sooner or later—no jury in the world would convict us."

As we approached the intersection of Allison and Lee, I saw another black-and-white unit parked in a gas station lot with its dome light on.

"There's the stupid sonofabitch now," D'Angelo growled. "Douche wouldn't make a good-sized pimple on a street cop's ass," he muttered to himself. We pulled alongside the other car. "Evening, Sergeant. Lovely night, ain't it?"

The man behind the wheel looked up from a clipboard on his lap. He seemed annoyed. A young, serious face. He looked like one of my students at the university.

"You're late," he said, glancing at his watch. "D'Angelo, I've just had a complaint on you."

"Me? Must be a mistake, Sarge. Some copper that looks a lot like me, I'll bet."

"This isn't a joking matter, D'Angelo," the sergeant snapped. He paused to examine a note in one of his pockets. "A guy named Robert Hartley, owner of The Candle Book and Novelty Shop out on West Main. He says you've been harassing him."

"Oh, that," D'Angelo said. "Care for a stick of gum, Sarge?"

"No, I would not," Sergeant Bernard said dryly. "Now, what did you do?"

D'Angelo waved a hand. "Aw, the guy's just pissed off 'cause I wrote him up for not having his business permit posted in plain view." He looked at Sergeant Bernard. "You know, like it says in the Municipal Code that every business is supposed to. I think it's Section Seventeen eighty-eight point six, but let me check it to be sure." He picked up our city code book and began thumbing through it.

"I know the code!" Bernard snapped. "I want to know what you were doing in there in the first place."

"Routine check of the premises, Sergeant." D'Angelo smiled. "Wasn't you at roll call tonight, sir? We're supposed to be covering Ninety-four till around ten."

"The owner of the store claims—now I want the truth, D'Angelo." Sergeant Bernard pointed a finger at my partner. Irritation was starting to creep into his voice. "He claims that you called him an 'asshole.' "

An exaggerated look of shock registered on D'Angelo's face. "He said I said a thing like that? To a fine upstanding citizen like him? Doc, tell him, did I call that asshole an asshole?"

"Uh . . . no! No, of course not," I said, immediately wondering why I had lied.

"He said that you went out of your way to embarrass him in front of his customers," Bernard said.

D'Angelo snorted. "How do you embarrass a slimeball like that, somebody that sells that kinda shit? He sells to kids, for Chrissakes. We oughta—"

"Dammit, D'Angelo," Bernard broke in, "if you've got something tangible, then call Vice Intelligence and give it to them. That's their job. Otherwise, stay the hell away from there. You don't have any business going in there making a scene. It's bad for community relations."

"Yessir. Is there anything else, Sergeant?"

Bernard shook his head. "No, that's all. Let's just not

make any more trouble than we have to, all right?" He started his car and pulled off.

D'Angelo watched him disappear in his rearview mirror. "Hell," he said as he started the car, "I was pounding a beat down here when that little bastard was still messing his diapers." He rode for several blocks without saying anything, then he added, "Before Douche come down here he never worked nothing but them crabgrass beats over on Southside. Getting cats outta trees, walking old ladies across the street—all that community relations garbage. That's all he can think of. Real crime fighter!"

At ten o'clock another unit began covering Beat Ninety-four and we returned to patrolling the ghetto. It was just before midnight when we made a right turn onto Washington Street and D'Angelo abruptly braked the cruiser. He put the car in reverse and backed up several yards, then sat motionless, staring into the darkness.

I looked around. I couldn't see anything. "What's the matter?" I whispered.

"Okay, come outta there," he ordered in a loud voice. He unsnapped his gun, resting one hand on its grip as he got out and stood behind the open car door.

I still couldn't see anything.

"Watch yourself," he said without turning to look at me.

I was out of the car on my side now, still wondering what he was talking about. He beamed a shaft of light from the cruiser's spotlight into an alley and brought it to rest on a pile of wooden fruit crates. I saw movement as two black figures stepped slowly from behind the crates and stood in the spotlight's glare. They began walking toward us.

"Watch the one on your right," D'Angelo instructed.

I could see them both clearly now for the first time— two black youths in their late teens. "What did they do?" I asked as I watched the pair approach us.

"Don't know," he said, still without taking his eyes

off them. "They was walking along being real cool back there. Then they seen us coming and ducked into that alley. On the car," he said simply to the man on the left as he walked up.

The man quickly assumed what is often referred to as "the position"—feet wide apart, palms flat on the car. I guessed it was not the first time he had been stopped by the police.

"Shake the other one down," D'Angelo instructed as he began running his hands across the first man's shirt and trousers.

I stepped from behind the door and called out to the second man, "Excuse me, but I'm going to have to ask you to put your hands on the car." I was a little embarrassed at having made such a request without really knowing quite why.

"Say what, man?" The figure came toward me with both hands in the pockets of a windbreaker jacket.

"I said—"

"He said to get your ass on the car! Now move!"

I turned and saw that D'Angelo's revolver was out of its holster, pointed directly at the man. The man's eyes grew wide as he saw the gun.

"And take them hands outta your pockets nice and easy! That's it. Now get on the car like that officer told you."

I started frisking the second man.

"Well, well. What we got here?" D'Angelo said. He reached deep in the first man's groin area and emerged with a small nickel-plated revolver. "How about the other one?" he asked as I finished running both hands down a pantleg. He began handcuffing the first man.

I stopped as I felt something soft and spongy in the man's left sock. "There's something in his sock," I said as I stood up, "but it's too soft to be a weapon of any kind. I think it's a plastic bag of some sort. Do you want me to run a records check on him before we let him go?"

D'Angelo looked at me with a puzzled expression on

his face. "What the hell you mean, 'let him go'?" he exclaimed. "Find out what's in that sock."

"We can't do that," I protested.

I was familiar with legal restrictions placed on the police. Under the Supreme Court decision in *Terry v. Ohio*, it had been legal for me to frisk the man's outer clothing for weapons in order to protect myself in light of the pair's suspicious conduct, but it would be illegal for me to go beyond that extremely limited "search" and examine the man's sock without first having actual grounds to make an arrest. D'Angelo's recovery of a gun from the other man had been legal only because he had first felt an object which any police officer would have good reason to believe might be a weapon. That had justified a search of the man's crotch. But a soft object beneath a sock? Surely D'Angelo must know the law, I thought.

"Here, keep an eye on this one," he said. He walked over to where the second man was still spread-eagled against the patrol car. He reached inside the sock and withdrew a plastic bag filled with small, tightly folded aluminum foil packets. "Smack," he said as he opened one of them and examined its contents. "Four, five, six decks. You're under arrest too, friend. Gimme your handcuffs, Doc."

I handed them to him as my mind connected the white powder and the street label for herion.

We transported both men to the city jail and booked them.

Once we were back inside the car D'Angelo looked at me and said, "Don't never hesitate to draw down on assholes like them two if they don't move when you tell 'em to. It's something they understand."

I said nothing.

"And another thing," he added a block later as we pulled into a drive-in restaurant for coffee, "don't never let a guy walk up on you with his hands in his pockets like that. If he'd had a roscoe inside that jacket, he could have blasted you before you had time to bat an eye. Happened to a sergeant out in Seventy-two a month or so ago, but he was lucky. Bullet just creased his neck."

A car hop brought us two cups of hot coffee. I sat there for several minutes, sipping mine slowly, not saying anything.

"Something on your mind, Doc?" D'Angelo said.

"Yes, there is, now that you mention it, Angie."

"Well, go ahead, get it off your chest."

"You know as well as I do that searching that fellow's sock back there was as illegal as hell, don't you?" I blurted.

"So that's it," he said as he unwrapped a cigar.

"You're damn right that's it," I said angrily.

He shrugged. "So it was illegal. So what?" he said as he lit the cigar.

"So what? My God, how can you say a thing like that? We're supposed to be police officers. If we don't follow the law, how can we expect anybody else to respect it?"

He took a deep gulp of coffee. "That what you think them two back there was doing, respecting the law?" he said. "If I hadn't noticed 'em acting so squirrely, you can be sure they'd of knocked over one of them all-night markets over on Allison by now with the heater the little guy had in his jeans. Maybe hurt somebody, killed somebody doing it."

"I'm not talking about that," I said. "I'm talking about making a patently illegal search, then turning around and using the illegally obtained evidence to justify arresting a man. Now, that's wrong!"

D'Angelo frowned, puffing on the cigar in silence for a moment. "Okay, Professor, let's analyze this situation," he said at last. "Let's say we done it your way—let the guy with the dope in his sock go 'cause we didn't have no legal grounds to search him. What then?" He leaned back in the seat and folded his arms across his chest.

"Then—"

"Then he'd be back down in the project pushing the shit in his sock next morning, wouldn't he? You heard the check that come back on both of 'em. They both done time for selling drugs."

"Sure, they're hoodlums, Angie. But that's got nothing to do with it. We're police officers. We can't go around like a couple of vigilantes meting out curbside justice. We—"

"Hey, don't talk to me about justice, Doc," he said. "I seen enough of it over the years down here." He crumpled the empty coffee cup and threw it out his window. "Justice, my ass! Like that trial downtown last week—the one of them three that dragged the guy outta his car over on Garfield. You follow it?"

I shook my head.

"Well, I did," he said. " 'Cause me and my partner arrested one of the bastards that done it. Let me tell you about it." He stared vacantly out his window for several seconds. "This guy was new in town, see. Colored guy. Worked as a shipping clerk somewhere. Anyway, one of his kids was sick and he was out driving around trying to find an all-night drugstore to get some medicine." He leaned forward and draped both wrists across the steering wheel. "He got lost and wound up down here. He's sitting waiting on a light when these three bugs come up and snatch him out from behind the wheel. They take him out to the city dump and rob him. He's only got three, maybe four bucks in cash on him. That ain't enough, see? They get mad. Tell him they're gonna kill him now." He looked at me. "One of the bastards later admitted in court that the guy pled with them, cried and all. Told 'em he had four kids. Begged them not to kill him. But they done it anyway, Doc. Shot him fifteen times in all—right after they made a tape recording of him pleading with 'em."

"My God . . ."

"And you know what they got?" he went on. "Only murder second for two of 'em, and the one that got murder first, they'll commute his sentence sooner or later—just wait and see if they don't." He started the car and we rode for several minutes without saying anything. "I could give you a hundred other cases just as bad as that one. You ever meet Charlie Dixon?" he asked.

"No, who's he?"

"Guy about forty. Works over in personnel. You can't miss him, he's the only one over there in a wheel-chair."

I remembered now having seen the man the day I filled out my personnel papers.

"Charlie's been off the streets for around three years now. He used to ride Ninety-one," he said.

"What happened to him?"

"One night he walked up on a stickup in that Shell station over at Fifth and Egan. He was just going inside to use the phone—didn't suspect nothing. Guy shot him in the back when he walked through the door. They say he won't never walk again. We thought he was going to die for quite a while." He stopped the black-and-white and watched a plate-glass window until we saw the clerk in a liquor store emerge from a back room.

"Did they get the man who did it—the one who shot Dixon?" I asked.

"Oh, yeah, we got him all right. He pulled around two years in prison. He's back on the streets now. In fact he knocked over a market on our beat just a week or so ago. We got a robbery warrant out on him right now." He reached over the visor and showed me a mug shot of the man. "So don't tell me about justice, Doc. Tell it to all the decent colored down here that're too scared to step outside their houses after dark, or try talking about it to Charlie Dixon, or maybe to the wife and kids of the guy that got murdered at the dump."

"But a policeman can't go around punishing crimi-nals just because the justice system doesn't work as it should, Angie! And punishment has never worked. History is a chronicle of man's inhumanity to man, all the way from the rack and thumbscrew to the electric chair. It's useless to—"

"Yeah," he said. "What about the guy who kicked you in the balls, the one we charged with resisting ar-rest? You don't want to see him punished?"

"I—"

"Well, let me tell you something: It don't matter none what you want. They won't do a thing to him. They'll either dismiss the charge or let him cop to disorderly conduct."

"Why should they do that?" I said. "Assaulting a police officer is a felony!"

"Why? I'll tell you why," he said. " 'Cause they don't care nothing about you. You're a cop, you're nothing. You'll learn that if you stick around long enough. The DA's office, the judges and jurors—they don't give a damn if you and me get our heads blown off out here. What they do care about is protecting the rights of punks like them two we arrested tonight. Well, I say fuck their rights! And fuck the courts too if they're too damn stupid to know the difference between right and wrong anymore! What about *my* rights? And Charlie Dixon's right? And the rights of the guy they found at the dump? Don't we have any? You're the professor, Doc. You tell me."

It was late and I was getting tired. D'Angelo, the avenging angel, I thought as we bounced onto a side street off Allison. What an odd couple we were.

"Hell, I know I got no case on that dope," D'Angelo said after a while.

"Then why—"

"Because at least we got that maggot off the streets for one night, didn't we?" he said. "Maybe it's just for one night, but I'll sleep better knowing we done that much. And no kids are going to be shooting that stuff into their veins at recess tomorrow."

He looked at me as we pulled into the station lot that night. "Doc, I like you. You're a nice guy, but you got a lot to learn about being a cop, and a lot more to learn about justice."

7

STREET COPS

A young black policeman made an unsuccessful grab at D'Angelo's hat as he came up behind us in the station parking lot.

"Don't touch me, boy!" D'Angelo protested. "That stuff comes off." He ducked and then lunged at the black officer, chasing him several yards.

"Hey, Doc, you better tell that old man to slow down. He'll have a heart attack sure!" The officer laughed as he looked back over his shoulder.

"Who you calling an old man? I can still whip your ass any day of the week, sonny!" D'Angelo shouted.

I laughed. We had been partners for almost two weeks now. I had begun to realize that there was something about the big policeman that I liked and respected, some intangible quality of self buried beneath the calculated roughness, the vulgarity and cigar smoke. That something made our frequent disagreements about crime and offenders less and less important as time went on. I had discovered during those first nights that the front seat of a patrol car is an inescapably intimate environment, a place where men come to learn a great deal about each other.

"Here, you drive tonight, Doc," D'Angelo said as he tossed me the keys to the black-and-white. "I'm getting tired of doing all the work."

I sensed I was being paid a compliment. Senior officers seldom allowed rookies as green as I was to drive the patrol cars that had been issued to them. I started the cruiser and felt the cool rush of air from the vents. The radio came alive. I shifted in my seat as D'Angelo picked up the microphone and checked us in service. The uniform and wide leather belt felt somehow less uncomfortable and awkward than it had at first. I returned the wave of two other policemen in a passing car as I nosed the cruiser into the street and felt it respond to the pressure of my foot. It occurred to me that the other men were gradually coming to accept me. Whatever reservations about my presence on the force they might still have harbored, the fact that D'Angelo seemed to accept me was good enough for most of them. That and the fact that I was out here in a uniform taking the same chances as everyone else.

"Now don't go getting a lead foot and stacking the thing up, Doc," D'Angelo said. "You rookies are all alike—hot dogs!"

There was so much to learn out here, I thought, and so little from my background and education that could be neatly and quickly applied to the problems I now faced as a working patrolman. A university professor is, in a very real sense, a kind of subsidized dreamer, someone who is rewarded by society for occupying himself with the abstract and the impractical, for avoiding those things that have to do with the here-and-now. The job of a policeman is diametrically opposite. It demands a constant and minute degree of attention to events in the real world. Even the most seemingly insignificant things quickly take on a new kind of importance for a patrolman—an out-of-place shadow, a barely discernible noise, a shifting glance, a cracked windowpane, a face and a car that somehow don't seem to match.

It was for this reason that "spacing out" (which D'Angelo referred to less charitably as "having your head up your ass") emerged as my biggest problem during those first weeks on the force. Time and again, my mind would drift off to this article or that theory as we responded to calls on our beat, or I would begin speculating on the demographic features of a suspect's background as we talked to him.

"Pull up over there, Doc," Angie said as we drove along West Allison. He pointed to the figure of a man curled up in the shadows beneath a billboard. "Sam . . . Sam, that you?" he called out.

The figure stirred as it propped itself against one of the billboard's wooden posts. We got out and made our way to it through the weeds and litter.

" 'Lo, Angie." The man coughed.

D'Angelo bent over and took a rag from a pair of bony hands. "Sam, I thought you was gonna leave this stuff alone last time we talked."

The man shrugged, flashed a toothless grin. He was old and black and his body reeked of sweat.

"Sterno," D'Angelo said simply as he stood and handed me the rag. Several more containers of the canned heat were scattered on the ground beside the man. They gave mute testimony to the fate of so many alcoholics in the ghetto, men and women who could no longer afford even the price of a cheap bottle of wine. Like the man in front of us, such people were often reduced to squeezing the pretty-colored—but eventually poisonous—Sterno into rags and then drinking the liquid residue. I looked at the purple, jellylike mass in the rag. The same thing that was used to keep trays of hors d'oeuvres warm at faculty parties back home, I thought. It was strange how everything down here seemed so turned around.

"Sam, what the hell am I gonna do with you?" Angie shook his head and handed the man back the rag. "C'mon, let's go. See you around, Sam," he said as we started toward the car.

"Shouldn't we have done something?" I said.

"Yeah? Like what?"

We got back inside the cruiser and I pulled out.

"I don't know," I said. "Take him to the hospital, or even lock him up. He'll kill himself sooner or later."

"Doc, I'll tell you something," Angie said as he adjusted the radio. "You can't stop a man—any man—

from killing himself if he wants to bad enough. You can maybe slow him down a little, but you can't stop him. Especially somebody like Sam back there. Life's already given him its worst shot. You can't threaten a guy who's really whipped—not with jail or nothing else."

We slowed to watch a black minister in a frayed white shirt and string tie as he preached from atop a car to people walking by. The radio was quiet now. It had been for several minutes. It got like that from time to time, but not often enough, I thought. I turned into one of the many narrow alleys running off both sides of the street.

"Po-lice! Help, po-lice!"

Angie and I saw the woman leaning against a brick wall in the glare of our headlights.

"I been robbed. . . . I been robbed!" she sobbed as we ran over to her. She looked at us with wild, frightened eyes. "Help me, please!" she said as we walked her back to the patrol car.

"What happened?" D'Angelo said calmly but with a trace of urgency in his voice.

She didn't answer but began rummaging in a large shoulder bag. "Oh, Jesus! He got my methadone! He took that, too!" she said as she raised a hand and brushed back several long strands of hair from a wig that was askew on her head.

Methadone. The word contained a wealth of information. It said that she was a narcotics addict, probably undergoing treatment in one of the clinics located in and around the project. Several minutes passed before we were able to calm her to the point where we could get a reasonably coherent description of the man who had robbed her.

I got back inside the black-and-white to put it out over the air while Angie pressed her for more details. "All units in the vicinity of West Allison," I began, "be on the lookout for a black male subject involved in a strong-arm robbery at Allison and Jarvis. Suspect is approximately five foot ten, one-seventy, last seen running—"

"Mister! Hey, mister!"

I looked up as I felt the woman's hand on my shoulder. "Stand by on bulletin," I said. I released the transmit button on the mike.

"He raped me, too," she said.

"What did you say?"

"I said he raped me, too," she repeated. I cast an incredulous glance at my partner, then sat there in confusion for several seconds with the microphone in my lap.

"Uh . . . Two Lima Ninety-five to all units . . . be advised that the suspect in the strong-arm robbery at Allison and Jarvis is, er . . . possibly also a rape suspect," I said.

The woman described how the man had raped her with infinitely greater calm than had characterized her earlier description of the loss of $38.40 and a bottle of methadone. "He say he want me to come up to his place for a little action," she began matter-of-factly. "He ask how much and I tell him. So we walk on over to his car in that parking lot on Jarvis. Then, next thing I know, he snatch my purse, then he say, 'Now you gonna give me some pussy, too!' He knock me down on the ground right there and take it."

At one point I said uncomfortably, "Miss, I'm sorry to have to ask you this, but we have to know. Did he . . . uh . . . did this man . . . did he ejaculate?" It would be critical in any hospital examination of the woman aimed at establishing the possibility of rape.

She looked at me uncomprehendingly. "Say what?"

"I have to know . . . if the man who assaulted you reached . . . you know, a climax?"

A puzzled expression.

"Did he come when he was inside you, ma'am?" Angie said as he looked up from the robbery report he was writing.

"Oh, yeah!" the woman said. "He come, sure enough!" She readily admitted that she was a prostitute and told us that she had had intercourse with at least five other men that night—"Five or six, I ain't sure which."

D'Angelo and I looked at each other. So much for the possibility of a medical examination. We finished taking the information for our report and offered her a ride back to the project address where she lived with her children. She thanked us but declined. D'Angelo explained to me that she could probably look forward to a beating from her pimp unless she somehow made up the money that had been taken in the robbery. I asked him how he felt about the rape of the woman in view of the fact that she was a prostitute.

"Way I see it," he said, "it don't make no difference that she's a whore. It's her ass, just like any other broad. She shouldn't have to give it to any guy she don't want to."

He was a strange man, I thought. Hard to understand, hard to categorize the way I had thought I might easily do when I first met him. Several blocks later we stopped a sports car that had run a light. We were just walking back to the cruiser after issuing the driver a verbal warning when we heard another car pull up.

"You men get those hats on right now! I'm getting damn sick and tired of telling you."

It was Sergeant Bernard.

"What difference does it make if we've got our hats on or off down here at this hour of the night?" I exclaimed to Angie as I watched Bernard drive off. "Doesn't he have anything better to do?" I added irritably.

"Doc, you gotta watch yourself," Angie said gravely. "You only been around two weeks and you're already showing signs of a real bad attitude. I'll have you know the rule about keeping them hats on is nothing less than a General Order!" He began chuckling. "Doc, we might just turn you into a street cop by the time you leave here. Yessir, we might just do that."

We handled several other calls that night before Angie finally said, "I'm hungry as hell. There's a little

burger joint over on Adams we ain't been to yet. Let's
eat, huh?"

We drove to the restaurant and parked the car just as
a newsboy finished stacking his papers in the coin stand
out front. We stopped in front of the stand and stared at
the bold headlines of the evening edition.

3 COPS ARRESTED IN GAMBLING RING

Angie stood there without saying anything for a minute.
Then he dropped a dime in the machine and removed a
paper. "C'mon, let's pick up a sandwich and eat in the
car tonight," he said.

I looked up and noticed that several people inside the
restaurant seemed to be watching us through the window. I felt a sense of shame as we got back inside the
black-and-white. Shame? Why should I feel shame? I
asked myself. I wasn't really a policeman. I stopped at
an all-night convenience store and waited while Angie
went inside for sandwiches. I picked up the newspaper
and read the article beneath the headline:

Chief of Police John T. Benjamin today an-
nounced the arrest of three officers in his department on charges that they provided systematic protection on several large gambling rings in return
for payoffs. Lt. Vincent R. Hartsfield, Sgt. George
A. Buie and Officer R. L. Ashborne were arrested
late this afternoon at the Vice Division office
where they worked by FBI agents and members of
the police department's Internal Affairs Division.
Both Hartsfield and Buie were fifteen-year veterans. All three policemen were apparently . . .

I stopped reading and put the paper down. All right,
I thought, so three policemen had been arrested. Three
out of a thousand. It wasn't fair for anyone to judge the
rest of us—Us? I caught myself on the word. Term de-
noting reference group identification, a voice in my

head said. Term suggesting feelings of peer solidarity. Us?

A few moments later Angie arrived with ham-and-cheese sandwiches and coffee. We parked across the street and I began unwrapping one of the sandwiches while he put on his reading glasses. They made him look much older. I guessed that was why he seldom wore them. He read in silence for some minutes and then put the glasses back in his shirt pocket.

"Did you know any of them?" I asked.

He nodded. "Buie and me was riding partners for a while, pretty good friends," he said.

"What do you think will happen to them?" I said.

He looked at me and I saw the anger on his face. "I hope they hang their asses—all three of 'em! The sonsabitches ought to rot in prison."

We sat there listening to the radio and eating our sandwiches without saying anything.

"I'll tell you something, Doc," he finally said. "I ain't got hardly a pot to piss in that I can call my own. But I sleep good at night. I ain't never took the first damn thing in this job that didn't belong to me. Not even back in the old days, before Benjamin took over, back when plenty of guys was stealing and shaking places down." He touched the shield on his chest with a thumb. "I ain't never used this for nothing but taking assholes off the street—not once in all these years! Not even to get a piece of some broad trying to get out of a ticket."

I looked at the badge's dull finish. The low number stamped on its face attested to the number of years its wearer had been a city policeman.

I was about to start the car when we both heard a sound breaking through the radio's silence. Another microphone keying intermittently. Gasps. Then a man's voice: "Signal Zero! . . . Seventy-six! . . . Sig—" Silence.

We sat there in the darkness for an eternity. Blind. Waiting. The emergency tone. A shrill female voice now: "All units! Officer needs assistance! Stand by . . ."

D'Angelo slammed a fist down hard on the dash. "Where? Goddammit, where?" he demanded.

"All units, be advised Motor Unit Two Kilo Seventy-six calling for assistance! Unit logged on a vehicle stop at Fourteenth and Julia."

The rest of the transmission from headquarters was lost as D'Angelo hit the siren. "Go!" he shouted.

I punched the accelerator and then hit the brakes. My mind was spinning. Cars screeched to a stop around us. "Which way, Angie? Which way?"

"Left at the light," he shouted over the siren.

I dug my nails into the steering wheel as we made the corner. Dear Lord, why had he picked tonight to let me drive?

"Faster, Doc! Kick it in the ass! Left up there!"

We're going to have a wreck! I can't drive like this, I thought as I pushed the gas pedal steadily forward. I wished now I'd told him what a poor driver I was to begin with.

"Faster! That's it! Cut over the line—go ahead, it's clear."

My heart was pounding in my chest, everything melting together in my mind. What was I doing out here? I swerved to avoid a bread truck that had stopped abruptly in the middle lane up ahead.

"Don't brake, don't brake!" D'Angelo shouted.

I started to glance down at the speedometer and stopped myself. Another six blocks and we careened onto Julia. We were almost there. I could see it now. The morotcycle unit's small rotating blue light. A white helmet on the ground. A man in a police uniform stood struggling beside a car with two white men. A loose circle of people stood around them. There was a terrifying sound of brakes and a smell of burning rubber as we came to a stop. Angie was out of the cruiser in a flash, running toward the other officer, grabbing one of the two men and tumbling backward onto the ground with him.

I felt something roll against my leg. A flashlight. I

grabbed it and jumped out of the car. The second man was pounding the motorcycle officer's head against the hood of a red car as I ran up behind him. A big man with thick black hair slicked back on the sides of his head. I raised the long flashlight and brought it down with all my strength on what I thought would be the beefy shoulder in front of me. But at exactly the same moment the motor man succeeded in knocking his assailant off balance, so the blow landed squarely in the middle of the man's head. He screamed in pain as batteries and pieces of glass from the lens scattered. Then he turned, half stumbled toward me and collapsed on the pavement.

Other police cars were now streaming down both sides of the street. Sirens. Lights. Brakes. The sound of running feet. I stood there, still holding the shell of the flashlight tightly, looking around at the crowd of spectators that had been watching the two men assault the motor officer. Most of them were white, male, young. Not one had tried to help.

"What the hell's wrong with you people?" I heard myself say.

They began walking off. A husky youth of about twenty averted his eyes from mine.

Us. That was the way it was most of the time, I would learn. I would come to realize that we really had only one another to depend on, only one another to call on in time of trouble. That was why each man put aside his own personal safety whenever an emergency call for assistance went out from another officer. That was why good men, normally careful policemen, threw caution to the winds. Drove like maniacs. Ran. Climbed. Did anything to get there. Get there fast! Officer needs assistance. One of your own was in danger. That was all that mattered.

Angie crouched over the man on the ground, who was now groaning and rubbing his head. The matted black hair was covered with blood. "Jesus, Doc," he said as he shook his head, "I'm afraid this is serious." He looked up at me. "That there light you just busted is

city property. Bernard'll want a Form Ten explaining
what happened to it. You might wind up having to pay
for it."

We arrested both men and transported them to jail,
after first stopping at General Emergency where the man
I had struck took an alarming number of stitches. Much
to my surprise, neither man had been a fleeing felon or
an ex-mental patient gone berserk. Just a couple of construction workers who had had a few too many drinks
when the motor officer stopped them for speeding. Neither one had ever been arrested before. I would find
during my months on the force that alcohol can trans-
form many otherwise ordinary, law-abiding people into
unpredictable and sometimes dangerous creatures.

"You might have to go up to Internal on this one,
Doc, but don't worry. Chuck and me seen the whole
thing," Angie said as we stood in the booking area filling out forms.

"Internal Affairs? What for?" I exclaimed.

"Aw, it's just the way them bastards up there are.
Every time you scratch somebody nowadays, they make
a big deal out of it." He began instructing me how to fill
out a Use of Force report form.

I looked at the form in front of me. Use of force?
How could I be sitting here filling out a Use of Force
report, trying to protect myself against a charge of police brutality? It wasn't my fault that the man had at-
tacked the motorcycle officer, was it? I hadn't meant to
hit him in the head.

"Doc, we're gonna have to go inside to get some
photocopies of these reports," Angie said. "Here, lock
the guns up." He unsnapped his revolver and handed
it to me.

The procedure was a simple one. I had been through
it a dozen or more times already. Because of the obvious danger of a prisoner inside the locked area of the
jail getting at an officer's gun, there was a regulation
that required each of us to secure his weapon in one of
the small metal lockers outside before entering the compound. You just put your revolver inside a locker, re-

move the steel padlock and key from inside, snap the lock shut and stick the key in your belt until you are ready to leave. Simple. Even a child could do it.

I was still thinking about the flashlight incident as I put both our guns inside a locker. Suppose the man filed brutality charges against me? Maybe I shouldn't have hit him. Maybe I should have done something else. I snapped the padlock shut. I had just turned away from the locker and started toward Angie when it hit me. The key! I'd forgotten to take the key out of the locker. It was locked inside with the guns!

Several minutes passed before I mustered the courage to speak. "Angie," I said.

"Uh huh." He continued working on a report page without looking up.

"Angie . . . I don't quite know how to say this . . . uh . . . you know the key to the gun locker?"

"Yeah. What about it?" he said. He looked up from the report.

"I really hate to say this, but I . . ."

"No . . . aw, no! Tell me you didn't, Doc!" he said with pained expression on his face.

"I did."

He buried his face in his arms on the booking counter and muttered something unintelligible.

There ensued a frantic hour during which we roamed about the jail compound searching in vain for someone with the master key to Gun Locker Seventeen. Seventeen. The number is seared in my mind for all time. We finally borrowed a hacksaw from one of the maintenance men at the jail, something that necessitated going through two of his supervisors first. No good. Angie spent almost fifteen minutes, red-faced and cursing, sawing and beating on the lock, while a growing number of trusties and jail personnel looked on with obvious amusement. The lock was barely scratched when he finished. He glowered at me.

"You know, the English have unarmed police," I said in a feeble attempt at humor. If he was amused, he didn't show it.

"Headquarters to Two Lima Ninety-five . . . are you in service from the jail yet?" the radio on my belt crackled. Several seconds went by. "Two Lima Ninety-five, do you copy?" the dispatcher repeated.

"Well, go ahead, you dumb shit," Angie said. "Why don't you tell 'em what you done!"

I picked up the portable radio. "Ah . . . Two Lima Ninety-five to Headquarters, be advised that we're still . . . uh . . . busy at the jail . . . will advise."

After some minutes of conferring with a correctional lieutenant at the jail and Sergeant Bernard, who had now also shown up to find out why we weren't back on patrol, a decision was reached: The fire department would have to be called to snap the lock off with a pair of bolt cutters. A call was placed and several minutes later we heard the sound of sirens approaching the jail as four pieces of fire equipment pulled into the compound. Through some confusion, the fire department had gotten the idea that there was a fire.

"Why me?" D'Angelo said. He looked up at the sky. "Why the hell me?" He said very little to me for the rest of that shift.

For days to come Angie joked about the flashlight incident—and I was embarrassed by it—as word of what had happened spread throughout the station. ("I'll tell you, the Doc here's a real terror. I gotta be pulling him off people all the time! Hell, he's already got a file a foot thick up at Internal!") As for what had happened with the gun locker, it led my partner to begin taking special precautions—like carrying an extra set of keys to the black-and-white for the first time in seventeen years, just in case I locked the others inside the car.

I resolved to double my efforts to stop "spacing out."

8

THE LESSON

FRIDAY night, June 29, 1973. Exactly a month on the force tonight, I thought, as I watched the passing streets.

"Headquarters to Two Lima Ninety-five . . . take a silent alarm. Rodriguez Furniture Discount, Nineteen-hundred South Blanding."

"Two Lima Ninety-five, ten-four," I replied. I turned to Angie. "Not another one," I said to him. "This makes the second one tonight. Hell, we've only been on two hours."

While I had reacted with tension and caution to the burglary alarms on our beat for the first few nights, I had gradually come to regard them as nothing more significant than barking dogs and stalled vehicles. A night seldom went by without our responding to at least one burglary alarm in Ninety-five. They were always false alarms: a rat triggering an invisible electronic beam, a drop of water from a leaky ceiling, a flash of lightning that accidentally activated a light on some dispatcher's console in communications. Angie had explained to me that most of the merchants around the project were either unwilling or unable to spend the money necessary for decent burglar-alarm systems.

Angie cut the cruiser's engine as we coasted to a stop with our lights out behind Rodriguez Furniture Discount. "I'll check the front," I volunteered.

He nodded and reached under the seat for the short twelve-gauge double-barrel he kept there. It was strictly against departmental regulations for an officer even to have one inside a patrol car, let alone carry it on a call. A man could get a two-week suspension without pay. But he knew that. It seemed he was always violating one general order or another, always being reprimanded or warned by Sergeant Bernard for something. I thought of the bullets in his gun—110-grain jacketed hollowpoints, better known as dumdums, another violation of departmental regulations. One night Bernard would check our guns unexpectedly and find them in Angie's .38, I thought. I had once asked him why he carried the prohibited ammunition.

"Only reason to ever fire this thing," he had said, "is to save my ass or somebody else's. I just want to make real sure I do it."

I left the department's twelve-guage Remington Wingmaster locked in its rack against the cruiser's dash as I got out and began walking around the building. I rounded the front corner with my flashlight in one hand, my revolver still strapped in its holster. I flashed the beam of light indifferently across the doors and windows as I walked along. I thought of my wife. The baby was due any day now. I was just waiting for the call that would put me on a jet for the flight home. I should be there right now, I thought, instead of out here playing po—

I stopped as something crunched under my feet. I shined the light down. Glass. My heart jumped as I looked up and saw the door in front of me. It was open several inches. I dropped and cut the light, listening now to the sound of my own breathing. The gun was in my hand. I squinted into the blackness of the store beyond the display windows. Nothing. I could just make out Angie's frame as it rounded the opposite corner with the short gun cradled across one arm. I pointed to the door and he waved an acknowledgment, crawling along the sidewalk until he reached where I was kneeling.

"Get us some help," he whispered quickly. It was the first time I had ever heard him whisper anything.

I cupped the portable radio close to my mouth and spoke in a hushed voice. "Two Lima Ninety-five to Headquarters . . . we have an open door on this silent . . . request backup." Within a couple of minutes another black-and-white glided to a stop. The two officers inside got out and joined us, one of them racking a shotgun as he came up.

Angie said, "one of you guys cover the back." The taller of the two officers disappeared around the side of the building. "Watch the front, Dave. We're going in," he instructed the man with the shotgun. The other officer nodded and took up a position next to one of the concrete walls.

Going in? What did he mean, going in? There was somebody *in there!*

"Doc, when we get inside, take the aisle on your right. I'll get the one on the left. Watch yourself," Angie said. He was creeping toward the open door before I could speak.

My throat felt dry. My palms were sweating profusely. I'm not going in there, I told myself. We should have waited for more units. There were other units on the way. Damn him, anyway! I felt my feet beginning to move reluctantly forward. Then I was inside the store, starting slowly along the thick carpet. My eyes darted quickly from side to side. Suppose he had a gun? Do most burglars carry guns? I wondered, realizing that the question was far from an academic one now. I recalled something Angie had once warned me about on a burglary call. I held the flashlight well away from my body as I turned it on so as not to provide anyone inside with a target. I kept my index finger tightly around the revolver's trigger. Suppose there was more than one of them? I licked my lips and inched forward, catching occasional flashes from Angie's light on the other side of the store. Nothing there. Or there. Maybe whoever had broken in was gone now, I thought hopefully. A noise. Down the aisle on my left. I stopped and listened, then slowly moved the light across an Early American secretary, a sofa.

"Don't shoot!" a man shouted as he sprang up like a jack-in-the-box from behind the sofa. I reflexively put several pounds of pressure on the gun's trigger as I pointed the weapon at the man and put my light in his eyes.

"Freeze!" I shouted. "Move and I'll blow your goddamn head off! Angie! Angie! Over here! Quick!"

"Where are you, Doc?" a voice called out in the darkness.

"Over here," I shouted again. I could hear my partner's feet pounding on the carpet as they came toward me. We search the man and handcuffed him as other officers began entering the store. One of them found a light switch and turned it on.

"Doc, I'm ashamed of you," D'Angelo said as we walked out of the store with our prisoner. "Was that you cussing at this guy back there, threating to blow his head off and all?" We started toward the black-and-white just as we heard Sergeant Bernard's voice behind us. I put the prisoner in the cage while Angie walked over to our supervisor.

"D'Angelo, I've had just about enough of your insubordination," Bernard snapped. He pointed at the sawed-off shotgun in one of my partner's hands. "You know you're not allowed to carry that thing. It's against reg—"

" 'Scuse me for interrupting, sir, but we got this prisoner to book. Oh, I guess you wasn't around, was you? Well, see, we had this burglary here an—"

"All right, mister. This one is going to cost you time off. I promise you that," Bernard said angrily as he stalked off.

We finished booking the prisoner and checked back in service.

"Bernard's an ass. How did he ever make sergeant in the first place?" I said. I looked over at D'Angelo as the lights of oncoming cars cast reflections across his face.

"That's what they want these days," he said. "Book guys like Douche." D'Angelo stared at the road ahead.

"I seen it coming for a long time now. Pretty soon good street cops will be gone—just like the dinosaurs. There won't be no place left for 'em to go."

I started copying an armed-robbery bulletin that was coming over the air as he spoke.

"It's all the weak sisters like Bernard, the new breed. They're giving up the streets, giving 'em back to all the punks and shitheads out here!" He slammed a palm against the steering wheel. "Every time I try to do my job, I wind up violating some rule that some pinheaded sonofabitch thought up over the last five minutes."

"Headquarters to Two Lima Ninety-five," the dispatcher's voice broke in, "a domestic disturbance at Four-fifteen Court Yankee, Apartment Seven."

I acknowledged and copied the address.

Angie went on. "Ten years ago, if you busted the law we put your ass in jail. It was that simple. We didn't sit around back then worrying about getting sued for false arrest, or being given days off, or maybe getting prosecuted for enforcing the law. We had a job to do and we done it." He turned onto Abraham as we headed for the family-disturbance call. "They say it was the old guys like me that put shotguns in the cars. That's bullshit! Hell, ten years ago I didn't even know how to use a shotgun. I didn't need to! No cop did, 'cause we had respect." He turned and looked at me. "It's guys like Douche that put shotguns in the cars, Doc, that started getting guys killed. It was them with all their community-relations crap that got every punk down here to thinking he could burn down the damn city every year and get away with it. It's them you can thank for being scared shitless every time you put that bag on."

We pulled over and heard the sound of an argument coming from an apartment building.

"Come on, Angie," I said, "you're just mad at Bernard. Most supervisors aren't like him. Look at Alt and Bennett and Hansen." All three sergeants were well liked and respected by the men on our watch.

"Yeah, I guess maybe I am," he said. We got out of the car and started up the walk. "I suppose maybe

Douche wouldn't be so bad if he hadn't had that there operation."

"What operation?" I asked. I knocked on the apartment door.

"You know," Angie said, "the one where they cut them slits in his gut. So he could still see with his head up his ass."

We both broke up laughing. It was a strange place to be laughing, but I had already learned that a policeman comes to savor humor whenever and wherever it is offered. It passes his way all too seldom. Angie and I would laugh other times as we recalled the imaginary slits in the young sergeant's waist. But we would never speak of the shotgun incident again, not even after he received a two-day suspension for having the prohibited weapon in his hands at the burglary.

We spent the next half hour trying to calm an angry man who was threatening to throw his wife's mother bodily out of the apartment when we arrived. We finally managed to settle all three parties down and left. Most people don't realize that for a policeman an arrest is always an instrument of last resort, something he uses reluctantly and only when he has nothing left to fall back on. He knows all too well that most arrests accomplish little if any good, especially in situations involving interpersonal conflict.

We returned to patrol. We were heading down West Allison when Angie stopped at the sight of another police car. It was parked in one of the traffic lanes up ahead with its blue lights rotating.

"You see that guy up there?" Angie said.

I looked at the policeman. He was standing beside his car and appeared to be arguing with a black man in another vehicle. "What about him?" I said.

"He's fucked up," Angie replied as he put the cruiser in park. He sat watching the other car.

"Why do you say that?"

"'Cause he hates anybody who's colored. He just can't keep from hassling 'em. Men, women, kids—it don't matter none to him. They're all just niggers.

That's what he's doing right now. Just messing with that guy for no reason. This ain't even near his beat."

The other policeman turned and saw our car now.

"Name's Bullock," Angie said. "He worked Ninety-five with me a few years back." He watched a number of people beginning to gather around the other police car. "We better wait till he gets the hell out before we leave. The guy's a riot just looking for someplace to happen."

"Why doesn't he work down here anymore?" I asked.

"'Cause I went and told the captain I wouldn't ride with the crazy sonofabitch no more. He's gonna get somebody killed sooner or later."

After several more minutes the other patrol car turned off its emergency lights and pulled away with a screech of tires. We continued driving down Allison and were about to stop for a cup of coffee when we heard the emergency tone followed by our car number.

"Oh, hell, here goes," Angie said.

I picked up the mike.

"Two Lima Ninety-five," the dispatcher said. "We have an unknown injury at Six-twenty-six Court Delta. Ambulance en route." I rogered the call.

Court Delta. Court Foxtrot. Court India. During my first days on the force I had naïvely assumed that these were actually the names of streets until Angie explained to me that they were just phonetic codes used over the police radio to differentiate a maze of alphabetized streets and courts running from A to Z in the project (spoken letters, like D, B, and E are easily misunderstood when used over the air, particularly in the kind of hurried transmissions often made by police dispatchers and officers).

"Okay, you tell me—which one's Delta," Angie said over the siren's wail as we pulled into the project.

I looked around for a familiar landmark. "Left up there, at the fireplug," I said. He nodded approval and made the turn.

Because of the lack of intact street signs in the Abraham Street project, I had begun spending afternoons in my room at the Raleigh carefully going over the beat map of Ninety-five, trying to associate different streets with particular landmarks: a partially torn-down car, an empty building, a regularly robbed market or drugstore, a billboard, the corner apartment of a chronically embattled husband and wife. I was getting better at finding my way around, but I wondered if I would ever know the terrain of poverty as well as Angie seemed to.

"Two Lima Ninety-five, arrival," I said as I cut the siren.

The ambulance had just turned onto Court Delta behind us. As we entered the apartment building, I saw a girl who looked as if she was about fifteen lying on her back in the hallway. Her face was contorted in pain and she clutched the worn fabric of her dress over her swollen abdomen. A middle-aged black woman knelt beside her, vainly trying to dispel the heat and flies with a newspaper.

"Oh, Mama! Mama, it hurts!"

"What happened?" I asked the black faces around me. An ambulance attendant began taking the girl's blood pressure.

"She fell down the stairs," the middle-aged woman sobbed. "Oh, baby, I told you to stay offa them stairs. There's too many bad boards on 'em."

"You're her mother?" I said.

The woman nodded, continuing to cry.

I hardly even noticed the dirt anymore, the smells and sounds of poverty. I crouched in the urine-spattered hallway and looked at the girl. During my first days as a patrolman I might have asked who her doctor was, or where her husband was. I knew better now, knew without asking that she had no husband and had probably never seen a doctor in her life. God, nobody should have to live like this, I told myself. Pushing a new life into the world in a filthy hallway. I thought of my wife, my own baby.

"Doc, give me a hand," Angie said. "These guys got a heart attack over on Fourteenth and they say that the shocks in that meat wagon out there are too rough for her. We'll take her in the cruiser."

I could tell from the girl's cries that the pains of hard labor were almost back to back now. Angie slid one hand under her back and another under her legs.

"Oh, please! Don't lift me, please!" she cried out. She clutched his uniform shirt tightly in one fist.

"Easy, now, honey. You're gonna be just fine," he said gently as he motioned for me to get the door. A strange tenderness came into his voice as he walked toward the car, still reassuring the girl. He eased her onto the back seat and got in after her, handing me the keys.

"Head for St. Luke's, Doc, it's closest," he said.

We pulled away with lights and siren.

A sharp cry of pain came from the back seat. I pushed the black-and-white faster.

"Listen, you got nothing to worry about. There ain't nothing to it. I oughtta know, my wife just had a baby," the voice in the back seat lied. "Just take it easy. You're gonna be okay."

"You're gonna be okay." As I listened to Angie I wondered how many times I had uttered that beneficent lie in the last month, uttered it in situations where I knew that things were far from okay, when I knew full well that the damage to another human being was already far beyond my meager curative powers. Reassuring people, I thought. Always reassuring other people and fighting to control the welling panic in yourself. It was strange. As the days and weeks in Ninety-five passed, I found myself deriving a curious kind of strength from nothing more than the apparent need of other people to believe in me. I discovered that people saw a policeman when they looked at me regardless of what I conceived of myself as being. And people in trouble have a desperate need to believe that just the presence of a policeman will somehow make things better, even people who despise what he represents. It makes no difference if the person who turns to you for help is a middle-aged matron pinned in the tangled wreckage of a car or a young black gang member lying in an alley with blood pumping from a knife wound in his chest. The illusion of omnipotence that they both invest in the badge and uniform is usually enough to carry you through, no matter how scared or inadequate you feel. The need never changes, nor does the lie. Just take it easy. You're gonna be okay!

We were approaching the intersection of Mayes and Tenth streets now. Only a few more blocks. I could already see the red light at the hospital's emergency entrance ramp.

"Oh, Mama! It hurts so bad!" A scream of pain.

Up ahead a car started into the intersection. "Don't do it, asshole!" I said aloud as I flipped the siren control from WAIL to YELP. I braked at the entrance ramp moments later and turned into the hospital. As I cut off the siren, I heard the distinctive squall coming from the back seat. The sound of new life.

"Angie . . . she didn't—" I turned and looked through the cage.

"She sure enough did, Doc! She sure enough did." He laughed.

I sat there watching the tiny figure on the back seat, wondering if the baby boy would grow up in the project, wondering if another policeman might one day have to take back the life we had helped give.

We spent the next fifteen minutes cleaning the back seat before checking back in service. Then a brief meeting with Sergeant Bernard, who returned our report on the furniture warehouse burglary to be rewritten. I had filled it out in blue ink instead of the black ink required by regulations. I drove now while Angie lit a cigar and started rewriting the report.

"Well, tell me, how does it feel to be a midwife?" I asked. I made a turn off Jefferson into Allison.

"Pretty much like it did the other three times," he said.

"My God! You've done this three times before?"

"Uh huh."

"One of us should run you in for practicing medicine without a license," I said. We both laughed.

Then we saw a late-model Pontiac shoot through the intersection we were approaching. I turned off Allison onto McKinley and accelerated after the car. "That guy's really hauling ass!" Angie said. The taillights were already receding far down the road ahead of us. I got close enough for a clock: fifty, sixty, seventy, in a thirty-mile-per-hour zone.

"I'll pull him at McKinley and Lee," I said.

Like so many patrolmen, neither of us liked working traffic. We were both inclined to give a driver the benefit of the doubt in the majority of situations, let a man have ten miles over the speed limit on a good safe road, or sometimes even coast through a stop sign if he was careful. But this was too much; this was the kind of driver who caused accidents that left people dead or seriously injured.

"Dammit!" Angie said. He sat holding the mike impatiently in one hand, waiting for a break in the almost continuous stream of Friday night air traffic, for a chance to advise headquarters that we were about to stop a green 1971 Pontiac Le Mans bearing license plate TNR-903 at McKinley and Lee. The girl sitting at the Zone Three communications console would then routinely teletype the number into a computer terminal link to both the state capitol and the FBI's National Crime Information Center in Washington. One of the modern wonders of law enforcement technology. We would have a check back on the plate in a matter of seconds in most cases.

"Two Lima Ninety-five to Headquarters, vehicle stop," Angie finally said.

"Two Lima Ninety-five, stand by. Two Lima Eighty-one, go ahead," the girl said.

"Shit!" my partner snorted.

I laughed. "Angie, I swear you're going to have ulcers before you're twenty."

"I already got 'em." He grinned. "And hemorrhoids too."

I flipped a switch on the dash and blue light bathed the car in front of us. The driver signaled and pulled over.

"Listen, Dr. Kildare, I'll catch it," I said. "Just wait here and run the plate." I got out of the car and began walking toward the Le Mans. A nice night for the end of June, I thought. There was a cool breeze starting to come out of the east, stirring bits of paper on the ground. The car window rolled down.

"Can I see your driver's license, please?" I said. I looked at the person behind the wheel. He was white, with pale freckles dotted across his nose and red hair neatly combed back on his head. Nineteen or twenty, I guessed.

"Evening, Officer." He smiled. Nice when people you stop smiled, I thought. Not that it would get him out of the ticket I had already decided to write, but it suggested that the whole thing might now be less unpleasant than it could be. "Look, I know why you stopped me, sir. It's my own fault," he said. "I'm late to work. I work at the cannery over on Palmetto."

"I'll need to see your driver's license," I said. I tucked the flashlight under my left arm and opened the citation book as he took out his wallet. "Son, you could have had an accident easily driving that fast," I continued, conscious that I really didn't want to write him a ticket that I knew would cost him thirty or forty dollars. That was a lot of money when you were nineteen or twenty, I reminded myself. "You were a good thirty-five miles over the posted limit," I added.

"Sir, I'm really sorry," he said earnestly. "Please, couldn't you let me go just this once? I've never had a ticket before."

I looked at him. Why not? I thought. Angie would probably be mad, call me a pushover, but what the hell? "Okay, I'm going to give you a break this time," I said, "but I'll still need to see your driver's license." I pointed to his wallet.

"Oh, sure! Sure! Let's see, it's here someplace," he said as he began rummaging through the billfold.

The breeze had picked up now. I turned toward it, feeling the rush of wind on my face as I waited for the license. I thought of the forthcoming meeting of the American Society of Criminology, at which I had been invited to present a paper on my experiences and observations as a scientist-turned-policeman. I would need a good title. Maybe something like—

"Freeze!"

I started, turning abruptly back toward the car. Angie was standing on the passenger side with his gun pointed through the open window at the driver.

"Wha—?" The man was bent over with one hand on the floorboard.

"Angie, what is it?"

If I had remembered to clip the portable radio to my belt I would have known, would have heard the emergency tone and the check that had just come back from headquarters on license plate TNR-903.

"I . . . I was trying to find my license," the driver said.

Angie cocked the .38 and braced it in both hands as he kept it pointed at his head. "Sure," he said, "go ahead and show the officer your license like you was going to. Go ahead," he shouted. The man brought his hands back to his lap. "Now get your mother-fuckin' hands on the wheel," D'Angelo ordered. "Car come back hot," he added without looking at me.

I drew my gun and opened the car door.

"Hot? You mean stolen, sir? There must be some mistake," the driver protested. I got him out and leaned him against the side of the Pontiac.

"Check under the seat," Angie instructed as he began searching him.

I took off my hat, knelt down and began groping under the front seat. My hand stopped as it came across checkered wood and cold metal. I pulled the object out and examined it. A .380 automatic. Full clip. Safety off. I pulled the slide back and watched a cartridge eject from the chamber and spin to the pavement. I felt weak, sick at my stomach. I leaned back against the car and started to tremble.

Angie said nothing, either on the way to the jail or during the full hour it took us to book the prisoner and inventory the stolen car. We rode in silence for almost thirty minutes after checking back in service before I managed to speak.

"Angie, I—"

"Don't say nothing to me!" he blurted. "You stupid goddamn intellectual! How many times I told you never to walk up on a car like that, huh? To always keep your eyes on a guy's hands! You got no business being out here. You're gonna get yourself killed, you know that, huh?" A deafening silence filled the car.

"I—"

"You oughta go back to that damn school where you belong," he said. "I'm tired of looking out for your ass!"

We talked no more for the remainder of the shift. I parked the black-and-white in the station lot and started to get out. He was right, I told myself. I didn't belong out here.

"Doc—"

I turned toward him.

"I blew my stack back there," he said. "I didn't mean all that."

"It's all right. I had it coming," I said quietly.

"No, you didn't. It was just as much my fault as it was yours. I done just what I told you never to do: I let you walk up on that guy while I sat back there with my head up my ass!" He sighed heavily, then rubbed his face. "It's just that we all get careless out there," he said. "I should know better after all these years, but I still do it. Things get so routine. That's what kills us."

I couldn't think of anything to say. We sat there.

"Angie."

"Yeah?"

"Thanks."

He grinned. "You got time for a quick one after we check off?" he said. I nodded.

I got drunk with D'Angelo that night, drunker than I can ever remember having been in my life, drunk enough to erase temporarily the memory of the brass cartridge ejecting from the automatic's chamber. The ultimate confession of inarticulateness, I thought drunkenly as I drifted toward sleep that night. A great leveler of men, the bullet. Like the grave, it takes no cognizance of a man's education or social position in life. The merciful numbness of sleep seized me.

The next night as I got ready to go on duty I opened the cylinder of my revolver and dumped the ammunition into a dresser drawer, replacing the regulation loads with six 110-grain jacketed hollow-points. Violation of General Order 7694.1, Sergeant Bernard's voice said in my head. "To hell with you and your General Orders, Douche!" I said aloud. I strapped the gun back in its holster and picked up my hat just as the phone rang. It was my wife's brother. They had just taken Merry Ann to the hospital, he told me. She was starting into labor. I called the department to leave word, changed clothes quickly and headed for the airport.

I got to the hospital back home a little before they wheeled her into the delivery room, and not long afterward found myself standing next to her bed looking down at a red-faced, healthy new son.

I spent the next week at home with my family, taking long walks by myself in the dense woods around our house, thinking about all the things I had seen and done, all the things that had happened to me during the past month. My wife was quick to notice the changes in me. I seemed so different, she said. Like some other person much of the time. Tense and restless, irritable. My language was incredibly profane. She could not recall ever having seen me take a drink to get to sleep at night. And why had I suddenly started sleeping with a gun beside the bed? Yes, of course it was ridiculous, I conceded. As a criminology professor I knew quite well that the statistical probability of my family being victimized by violent crime so far out in the country was small indeed. Still, I slept with the gun on my nightstand all during that week at home. I also bought my wife a gun and made her promise to keep it nearby at night while I was away and always to check the doors and windows carefully before she went to bed.

"Honey, honest to God, you're getting downright paranoid," she exclaimed one afternoon just before I left when workmen arrived to install burglar-alarm system in the house.

I smiled. "Just chalk it off to a little case of occupational disease I've come down with lately. Humor me like you would any other paranoid," I said.

It suddenly occurred to me how a clinical psychologist's evaluation of me might read at this point in my new career:

Patient is a thirty-one-year-old university professor currently working as a policeman. On examination, patient reveals unequivocal symptoms of paranoid ideation, most evident in the recurrent fantasy that he is surrounded by dangerous individuals and situations much of the time. Patient seemingly devoid of sentiments of trust and open-mindedness which others associate with his past life. Diffuse, free-floating anxiety centering around obsessive preoccupation with the possibility of physical attack and injury by others. Administration of Minnesota Multiphasic Personality inventory reveals a profile remarkably congruent with other police subjects studied. . . .

9

BLACK MAN

ALMOST three months in Ninety-five. I stood outside the assembly room with Angie and a black policeman named Franklin Griffin.

"Now you listen heah, boy," the Italian began in an implausible southern accent, "don't go messin' up all the hard work I put into the Doc here!"

The black policeman grinned. He racked open a shotgun and checked the breech. "Doc," he said, "if you've had enough of listening to Lard-ass here, I guess we can hit the bricks and do a little police work."

"Good. I was beginning to worry that I might never get rid of him." I smiled.

"Aw, to hell with both of you!" Angie said as he walked off.

A new partner, I thought, as we headed for Griffin's cruiser. I liked the young black man immediately. During the past several months he had been working Ninety-five on the day watch, along with a lanky Georgian named Ozman, while Angie and I covered the same beat at night. Now he and Angie would be trading places. I needed some experience working with another officer, the captain had said a few days earlier. He made the change of assignments effective today.

"Two Lima Ninety-five, in service," I said as Griffin started the car. "With Kirkham, Badge Ninety-twenty-seven, and D'An—correction, Headquarters—second officer, Griffin, Badge Eighty-six-fifteen," I continued, thinking that it was strange starting the shift without the big Italian next to me. D'Angelo and Griffin. The two men provided a dramatic contrast in stature. Franklin Griffin was unquestionably the shortest officer on the squad, while D'Angelo was one of the tallest. Indeed, the pair reminded me of Mutt and Jeff whenever I saw them standing together.

Griffin had once confided to me that he was almost a full half inch below the minimum acceptable height for police officers in our department and had only managed to join the force, after months of fruitless exercising and stretching, through a ruse. On the morning of the scheduled police physical examination, he had cut two thick wedges of leather from an old boot, glued them to his bare heels, and then put on heavy winter socks. Once he succeeded in conning a young nurse into letting him leave his socks on because the floor was so cold he was able to register a fraudulent five feet nine inches.

While several studies suggest that the probability of a police officer's being assaulted in the line of duty is closely associated with the factor of height (taller officers are supposedly safer), Franklin Griffin's body served amply to compensate for his short stature. Several years of semiprofessional boxing, weight lifting and street fighting in the very ghetto that he now patrolled had left him with a thick, powerful build. I looked at him as we started out together that first night. His skin was a deep lustrous ebony that set him apart from the countless shades of chocolate brown I had come to associate with the people of our beat. His nose was broad and flared at the nostrils. His hair was cropped close to his head, and his forehead seemed to be perennially furrowed.

"Two Lima Ni-yun fi-yuv . . . be advised we have no wants on current Juliette Whiskey November Fi-yuv ni-yun thur-ee," a voice carefully enunciated as the check came back on a car we had begun following on Garfield Boulevard.

"New dispatcher," I said.

Griffin nodded and smiled.

I guess that the girl on the other end of the radio was probably manning the Zone Three communications console for the first time tonight under the watchful eyes of a supervisor. The invisible women, I thought. They were our eyes in a very real sense, for we had to depend on them time after time each night to tell us everything possible about the kinds of calls we were about to walk up on. We accordingly blamed them, bitterly denounced them to each other, when the information they gave us proved to be wrong or incomplete or when they were too slow to respond to our requests. ("Come on, bitch! I ain't gonna follow this car all night!" Angie would explode.) Hapless females. We took it all out on them so many times, all the tension and anger we built up handling other people's problems. Perhaps we did so because the alternative was to begin venting aggression against each other, and men who have to depend on each other night after night for their very lives can't afford to do that. Looking back, I suppose we were so often hard on the faceless women just because of the fact that they were women and we were men. The inescapable truth was that here was a bitch goddess who held our fate in her hands every night, who decided when we could or could not eat dinner or stop for coffee, who nightly ran us around the small grid of our beat like some schoolmistress sending boys on errands. If men generally resent being supervised and controlled by members of the oppsoite sex, this is doubly true in police work, for it represents perhaps one of the last bastions of traditional masculinity in American society, a man's world in an era of steadily increasing unisexuality in most jobs, a place where the things that men do are still different from the things that women do, a place where the male animal's physical prowess still counts, at times.

Even the walls of this once sacrosanct male preserve were starting to crumble by 1971. There were already six women enrolled at our police academy in the summer of that year, each of them destined for patrol duty on the streets. I remember once asking Angie how he felt about the prospect of having a female partner. "I ain't gonna have no broad in my car," he had roared. "The day they stick me with a broad, that's the day I tell the old man where he can shove this piece of tin!"

Franklin stopped at a light alongside a pale white prostitute. "Hi, Sylvia, how's it going tonight?" he asked.

"Slow but it's still early," she replied with a blank look.

The dyed black hair and parchment-yellow skin made her look far older than I guessed her actual age to be. It occurred to me as I looked at her that she might once have been pretty. It was hard to tell. The heroin she was addicted to and several years as a prostitute on West Allison had ravaged whatever beauty had once existed. Life was hard enough for any woman in the ghetto who used her body as a means of survival, but it was especially difficult for a woman like Sylvia. A white woman in an all-black world. I thought of her pimp as she walked off, a muscular black who went by the street name of Hogshead. He had a reputation for gratuitous cruelty to the girls in his stable. Often we would see Sylvia with a black eye or a bruised face as we cruised our beat. Yet she continued to remain with Hogshead. He was her man, she said. I had begun to realize during the past three months how very little I really knew about human behavior, how little a doctoral degree teaches a man about life, about himself.

I waved as we drove off. We had a policy with girls like Sylvia. We did not bother them so long as they stayed clear of other forms of street crime. We left Sylvia and the other streetwalkers for the Vice Division to worry about, if only because there were just too many other more serious things to occupy a patrolman's time and attention on a beat like Ninety-five.

"She's a sad case, huh, Doc?" Franklin said.

I nodded, then began chuckling to myself as I remembered something.

"What's so funny?" my partner asked.

"Did Angie ever tell you about the time we rousted Sylvia and Hogshead over the TV?" I asked. He shook his head. "Well, we spotted both of them lugging this huge TV up a back staircase one night over on Carlton. Naturally, we figured it was hot. We're sitting in the car just watching where they take it when Angie starts ranting and raving—you know how he gets," I said.

The black policeman smiled. "Oh, I know how he gets," he said.

" 'Lookit that low-life bitch, Doc,' " I began in an imitation of the Italian's voice. " 'Up there screwing that goddamn nigger every night!' " I turned toward Griffin, who was chuckling. "I didn't realize it," I continued, "but my knee was resting against the mike's transmit button the whole time he was talking. The whole damn zone could hear us! Oh, God, did Douche ever chew us out!"

We both laughed, and then it dawned on me that I would never have considered telling a black person something like that a few months before. But things were different out here. Griffin's skin color didn't matter. The badge was all that mattered. We were both policemen.

"Doc, I hear Angie's got you carrying hot loads and wearing a vest. You're not getting paranoid on us, are you?" he said.

"It's not that, Franklin. You think I personally care about getting killed out here?"

"A guy could get that idea."

"It's not that at all. It's not my ass that I care about. It's just that I keep thinking about the terrible loss to science if anything should happen to me." We laughed.

Science, I thought. It was strange, but I hadn't thought of myself as a scientist in a very long time now. Sometimes it seemed that I had been down here in Ninety-five for years instead of months, that I would always be here, would grow old on the beat. Much to my surprise, an irrational part of me had begun to want to stay, to abandon the professional career which I had spent most of my life preparing for. Part of me had begun to crave something about the life I had known since the beginning of the summer: the tempo of the beat, the recurrent excitement, the high-pitched emergency tones over the radio that sent adrenaline surging through my veins with a mixture of fear and anticipation. The contest of wills, minds and bodies, the challenges, even the ubiquitous morbidity of the job seemed somehow to infect me. I was beginning to like being a policeman.

I ran two fingers underneath the tight blue collar. Summer was over. The temperature was still hovering in the high eighties as we went on duty, yet officially summer was over for the police department. Someone in the hierarchy of command had said so two days earlier and had ordered us to abandon the light, open-collared shirts in favor of long sleeves and clip-on ties (a patrolman never wears anything but a clip-on tie because of the obvious danger of having a conventional tie suddenly transformed into a weapon of strangulation). Perhaps a deputy chief, I thought, or even the old man himself. Angie had ascribed the premature shift to heavier uniforms, like almost every other evil visited upon us, to the malevolence of Sergeant Bernard. It was Douche who had personally drafted the most mindless and idiotic of the General Orders, Douche who engineered the assignment of involved calls to the members of A Squad during the last five minutes of the watch, Douche who was responsible for the poor maintenance of the black-and-whites.

"Hey, Franklin, swing by Feinstein's for a minute," I said. We parked in front of a small grocery store on the southwest corner of Allison and Ford. "You want one?" I asked my partner as I started to get out.

"Don't tempt me, Doc. I'm trying to cut down," he said.

Stopping at Feinstein's Grocery had become one of my regular patrol rituals. It ranked just behind what Angie referred to as "a coupla belts after shift—just to unwind." As I approached the front door of Feinstein's I noticed the slight but unmistakable paunch pressing against the Sam Browne. I was starting to gain weight for the first time in my life. Almost fifteen pounds in three months. My two-bag-a-night habit at Feinstein's didn't help, I told myself as I walked inside.

"Ah, Dr. Kirkham," the old merchant called out as he saw me.

"Hi, Alex," I said, thinking that he was the only person in the city who called me that. It always had an unfamiliar ring to it, somehow. Dr. Kirkham and Doc had become two separate identities housed in the same body, like Dr. Jekyll and Mr. Hyde.

I watched while Alex Feinstein scooped the hot nuts into two small brown paper bags. During my first days on the beat I had persisted in fishing in my pocket for change while the little man behind the counter protested vigorously. "No . . . no, please! No money from you boys," the pinched face behind the wire glasses would insist each night, until I finally took Angie's advice and abandoned my efforts to pay. In time I managed to stop worrying about the fact that accepting the nuts each night was a violation of a departmental order dealing with gratuities. "I got nothing but respect for that old Jew," Angie had once said. "It takes a ration of guts to run a store down here."

"Thanks, Alex," I said as I took the bags. Twenty years on West Allison, I thought, and he was still here. Neither the riots several years earlier nor the not-infrequent robberies and burglaries at his store had pushed the tenacious little merchant and his wife off their corner.

"So how's the baby," he said, coming out from behind the counter.

"A giant! Merry Ann says I won't even recognize him by the time I get home." We talked for a few minutes as usual before I left the store.

Franklin and I continued driving down Allison, looking at faces, windows, cars, at the myriad of things that policemen learn to watch.

"Hey, Chickee baby!" Franklin called out his window. He whistled as we passed two of the street's more conspicuous transvestites. We tried to keep a close eye on the many "he-she's" that abounded on West Allison and the blocks around it. We knew from experience that the men dressed as women were more likely than regular prostitutes to get involved in serious crimes like mugging and armed robbery. They were also more apt to become victims of crime themselves. Indeed, I had already seen several beaten badly, and one stabbed to death, by men who had groped in drunken anticipation beneath a skirt only to discover the wrong biologic equipment.

"I don't recognize the one on the left," I said.

"That sweet thing, Doc, is Chi-Chi. I busted her, him, or it last month on days. Traffic warrants," Franklin said.

"Headquarters to Two Lima Ninety-five . . ."

"Two Lima Ninety-five, ten-four," I replied, thinking that I detected hesitation in the dispatcher. You soon got so you could read things like that in the voices coming from the console.

"Two Lima Ninety-five . . . we have unknown trouble . . . Sixteen-fourteen Court Ocean."

I rogered the call. Unknown trouble. That was the kind of call we each dreaded most. Maybe just a senile old woman upset because children had been playing on her porch, or maybe a sniper crouched in one of the blackened project windows, waiting. You never knew which. Someone had called for The Man, given an address and then hung up. That was all you ever knew for certain.

"See that field, Doc," Franklin said a few minutes later as we drove into the housing project. "We used to live right there. Used to be an old apartment building standing there. They tore it down a couple years back after my mama moved out."

"How does she feel about you being a cop?" I asked. I remembered that he had once told me that his mother worked in a clothing shop on the other side of town.

"Oh, I guess you could say she's kind of proud of it," he said. "It's mostly my wife who's always on me to quit." He looked out his window at the passing build-

ings. "I guess I can see her side of it," he said. "It gets
pretty rough on her. Seems like about every time we go
anyplace lately, I wind up running into a dude I've
busted for something. A couple of times I've had to
duke it out right there in a movie or a store. It really
upsets her."

"It must be a lot different for you than the rest of us,"
I said, immediately thinking that it was a naïve thing to
say and wishing that I hadn't said it.

"Different? You're not kidding it's different! Listen,
Doc, you guys carry guns off duty mostly just because
the departments says we're supposed to. A black cop
carries one because he's got to. You don't so much as
dare to take a leak in a gas station or run down to the
store for a quart of milk without a piece stuck under
your shirt." He shook his head. "One night I even had a
couple dudes pop a cap at my car when I had Jan and
the baby in it."

"Why don't you quit? You must have thought about
quitting?" I said, recalling that he had once told me this
was his third year on the force.

"Yeah, I've thought about it, lots of times," he said.
"I'm only a year short of my bachelor's in psych. Jan's
old man offered to loan me the bread to finish up when
we got married. How about that, Doc? Land a nice
eight-to-five job in some office with twice the pay and
none of the crap we put up with out here."

I adjusted one of the cruiser's spotlights and saw the
address we were looking for. Just an argument, I
thought, with a sense of relief. I heard the sound of angry voices coming from an open window.

"Sometimes I don't know why I stay," Franklin said.

A middle-aged black woman stuck her head out of
the door as we walked up. "Good," she said, "I'm glad
you here."

She stepped aside and motioned for us to come in. As
we walked into the living room I noticed a picture of
Martin Luther King on one wall. The words "I have a
dream" were inscribed just above the civil-rights leader's face. An insect scurried across the wall beneath it.

"Jest you get him outta here. I want him outta this house now!" She pointed at a shirtless youth of about eighteen who stood cooking bacon and eggs on an old gas range. The boy turned and looked at us.

"Who is he?" I asked.

"You didn't have no call to go get the po-lice, Mama," the youth said as he turned a piece of bacon in the skillet.

"This is your son?" I asked as Franklin walked over to the boy.

"Yeah, he mine, but he ain't no good! He been stealing from me. I ain't gonna put up with it no mo'."

"How 'bout letting me finish my dinner first, Mama?" the boy asked as he scraped the eggs and bacon onto a plate.

"No! You git now!" she shouted.

"You old bitch!" He threw the fork he was holding at her.

"Okay, man! That's enough," my partner said, locking two brown hands on the slender wrists. "Now you can either leave on your own right now or you can come with us. Which is it?"

The boy hesitated for a moment. "I'll go," he said, taking a dirty T-shirt off the back of a chair and slipping it over protruding ribs. "Bitch!" he shouted back over his shoulder as he went through the front door.

A mother and her son, I thought to myself. I shook my head and looked at Franklin. My God, what this place did to the people in it! This monstrous human tragedy that we social scientists so blandly call an "ethnic socioeconomic environment." We left the woman's apartment. As we went back on patrol, I found myself wondering where the boy had gone to live.

Franklin pointed to a boarded-up building once we were back on West Allison. "See that, Doc?" he said. "That used to be the Roxy Theater when I was a kid. They used to have these things they called Saturday Specials every week. You could get in for just a quarter if you had two RC bottle caps." He laughed. "That was the catch. My little brother Ralph and me used to get up real early every Saturday and start combing the blocks looking for the damn things. They were hard as hell to find for some reason. It seemed like you could find just about every kind of bottle cap under the sun on a Saturday morning except an RC. I guess that's why they wouldn't take anything else."

"Was the project much different back then?" I asked.

"Oh, yeah—at least in some ways," he said. "You think it's rough down here now, you should have seen the blocks back when I was a kid. Man, they were wide open back then. Lots of the old places are closed down now." He paused and lit a cigarette. "I remember one night my mama took me shopping with her," he went on. "I was just a little guy—five, maybe six. We were walking past a bar called Filo's over at Jefferson and Ivy—it's gone now. Anyway, here's this bartender dragging a drunk outside. He dropped him in the gutter, then he pulled this little pistol out of his back pocket and stuck it against the guy's ear. I'll never forget it. It had a white handle. He just blew the guy's brains out right there in front of us. Then he stuck the gun back in his pocket and walked inside like nothing had even happened. Everybody just went on minding their own business. I started to scream and cry something awful, but Mama just dragged me off. 'Hush, Franklin. You hush up now!' I can still hear her saying that."

"Did you ever get in trouble with the police when you were growing up in the project?" I asked.

He laughed. "Did I get in trouble with the po-lice? Doc, is the Pope Catholic?"

We made a turn on Washington.

"Sure I did," he said. "Everybody did. You didn't grow up down here without getting in trouble with The Man."

"How'd you wind up wearing that instead of becoming one of the bad guys?" I asked him.

"Listen, it was a lot closer than you'd think," he said. "I guess I might have wound up in the joint if it hadn't been for Eb. He was an old black cop in the project when I was growing up. He's dead now." He shook his head and smiled. "I must have thought he was God Himself. We used to call him Big Eb down on the blocks. I guess he was close to six-five, weighed around two-forty."

Franklin's face brightened as he went on.

"He had this way of looking at you. You just knew for sure that he could read your mind. He was always catching me pulling some kind of shit—busting out windows, fighting, breaking into cigarette machines. One time he caught me hot-wiring a car when I was twelve. Did he give me a whipping! Mmmmmph!" We slowed to watch two black teen-agers who were loitering in front of a store window. "But he never busted me," he said. "He'd knock the hell out of me, then take me home to Mama, and she'd give it to me all over again." The boys in front of the store saw us and drifted off down the street. "Mama was tough. Maybe as tough as Eb himself in her own way."

As he spoke I began copying a bulletin on two men who had killed a highway patrolman in another state and were believed to be headed toward our city. Franklin paused, listening to the description, then continued.

"I remember one time right after I started first grade at Jefferson School. A big kid named Freddie Hansen, a third-grader, walked up to me and took the nickel Mama had given me for lunch milk. Then he knocked me down and said I'd better have another nickel tomorrow or he'd whip my ass. It was always that way in school. You even had to pay protection to the big kids to swim in the project pool."

"Did you give him another nickel?" I asked.

"I couldn't," he said. "When I went home crying and told Mama what had happened, she knocked hell out of me. 'You ain't getting no money tomorrow, boy! Now you make him give you dat nickel back or you ain't never gonna get no mo'!' " he mimicked. A sadness came across his face. "You know, Doc, I didn't understand what she was doing back then. I guess maybe I even hated her for not giving me the nickel next morning, but she knew you had to get tough in the project early to make it."

Survival, I thought. That was what everything in Ninety-five ultimately boiled down to.

The emergency tone. "Headquarters to Two Lima Ninety-five . . . major injury accident . . . Abraham and Court India . . . ambulance en route." We rushed back toward the project with blue lights and siren. By the time we arrived, a large crowd of people had gathered in the street around the form of a small boy. We got out of the car and pushed our way through the throng.

An elderly black man came up to us. "It wasn't that man's fault," he said as he pointed to a white man who stood beside the boy looking visibly shaken. I knelt and looked at the child. He looked about ten, about the age of my son Craig.

"I seen the whole thing!" the old man said. "These here kids was just funnin', runnin' back and forth in front of cars, seeing who could come closest to getting hit."

The ambulance attendants were beside us now, unsnapping a case, working quickly, quietly. A lone tennis shoe was lying on the ground several feet from the boy. There were some calls a man just couldn't get used to, couldn't find ways to insulate himself from. This was one of them.

"Tommy! Tommy! That's my brother!" a child's voice shouted from the crowd. Franklin caught a boy of about seven by both arms as he rushed forward. "Let go! He's my brother!" the boy sobbed.

"Hey, listen, he's going to be okay," Franklin said. "But you've got to let them help him. They're going to help him, hear?" The lie again, I thought. The same lie over and over again.

After we finished helping the attendants put the unconscious boy on a stretcher and place him in the ambulance, I noticed the hand I had held behind his head. It was wet and sticky with blood.

"Well, there's one it looks like we won't have to worry about," a voice said.

I turned and looked at the white policeman behind me. I had seen him before: Bullock, Angie's one-time partner, the one he had gotten transferred out of Ninety-five. The look on Franklin Griffin's face told me that he had heard Bullock's remark. He left the crying boy with a woman in the crowd and walked over to the other policeman.

"You're a little off your beat," my partner said.

Bullock smiled tightly. "Just thought you might need some help handling the natives," he said.

I saw the anger in Franklin's face as he spoke. "Do me a favor, Bullock."

"Anything for you, Griffin."

"Get the hell off my beat!" The two men glared at each other for a moment. Then Bullock turned and walked off. Franklin and I finished taking the necessary information for our report; then we went on to the hospital, where a nurse told us that the boy who had been hit had just died in surgery.

"Franklin," I said, once we were back in the cruiser, "for what it's worth, I think everybody feel pretty much the same way about Bullock. Angie says he's got no business being a cop, and they used to ride together. Every officer I've ever talked—"

"Talk!" he said. "That's about all anybody ever does when it comes to Bullock. Nobody ever does anything to get rid of the sonofabitch!"

"You've had trouble with him before?" I said.

He turned in the seat and looked at me as he spoke. "A few months after I got out of the academy, I was working one night when we had a robbery go down at the bus station. Headquarters put out a good description on both the car and suspect right after it happened. Next thing I know, I see Bullock, off his beat like always. He'd stopped a car driven by a guy named Jackie King over on Jefferson. Now I know Jackie real well. We grew up together. He's straight as a stick, owns a little carpet-laying shop over on Palmer. He's never

even been arrested in his life." He paused to shake a
cigarette out of a pack on the dash and light it. "Jackie's car and physical description weren't even close to
the suspect's, but that didn't matter to Bullock. He
wants to kill a nigger so bad he can taste it," he said
acidly. "He was standing there beside the cruiser with
Jackie when I pulled up. Doc, the guy went crazy! He
snatched him out and slammed him against the side of
the car, started calling him a no-good nigger. Before I
could get over there, he'd hauled off and smashed him
in the face with a shogun butt. Jackie didn't do anything
the whole time, just stood there with his hands up."

The black policeman slumped in his seat, drawing
smoke deeply into his lungs. "So I go running over to
Bullock. Jackie's there on the ground with a busted jaw
and Bullock's handcuffing him, still cussing him out,
asking him where the gun and money are. I tried to tell
him that Jackie couldn't be the guy, that I know him.
About that time one of the Southside units comes on the
air and says they've got both the suspect and money in
custody." He loosened his tie and unbottoned his collar.
"Then Bullock starts telling me he's real sorry, says he
made a mistake, but that he still has to arrest Jackie
King and charge him with resisting, to protect himself
in case Jackie decides to file a brutality complaint.
Jackie's lying there looking up at me. Bullock starts giving me all this crap about us being brother officers,
about how he could lose his shield for butt-stroking an
innocent guy. Some of the other guys showed up. They
said the same thing: Sure, Bullock was a bad cop, but
he was still a cop. We had to protect our own kind." He
looked at me. "Well, what about me, Doc? What did I
owe my own kind?"

He threw his cigarette out the window. " 'You tell
'em what happened, Franklin! Man, tell 'em what happened!' Jackie kept saying as Bullock put him in the
car. Well, I didn't tell them, Doc. I didn't tell them a
damn thing. When I got called in by Internal, I lied just
like the others—lied to protect the bastard! I don't
know to this day why I did it, why I didn't tell the truth.

Maybe it was just because I was a rookie. Maybe I had to show the rest of the guys just how white I could be, or maybe I just didn't have the guts to stand up and do what was right." He ran one hand across his forehead. "Jackie King hasn't spoken to me since that night, and you know something, Doc? I can't really blame him."

10

FULL MOON

I looked through the cruiser's windshield at the bright moon hanging in the evening sky over the housing project.

"We're in for it tonight, Doc," Franklin said.

"Maybe," I replied, "but it doesn't look quite full to me."

Franklin squinted for a moment. "No, it's full all right," he said. He followed his pronouncement with an imitation of a wolf's howl.

At first I had scoffed at Angie's assertion that a full moon was a sure sign that there would be trouble on our beat. But as time went on, my experience seemed to bear out this bit of police locker-room lore. It did indeed seem as if our worst nights—those nights when a continuous series of emergency tones sent us rushing from call to call—occurred when the moon was at its fullest. I smiled to myself as it occurred to me what my colleagues back at the university would make of such an unscientific idea. Still, I too began to rely on the moon's appearance as a barometer of trouble. Next you'll be believing in demons and werewolves, I told myself.

The emergency tone. "Headquarters to Two Lima Ninety-five . . ."

"Two Lima Ninety-five, go ahead," Franklin replied.

"Two Lima Ninety-five . . . armed robbery with in-

juries just occurred at Sixty-seven-eighty-nine West Allison."

My heart jumped as I heard the address. I had seen
the numbers a hundred times or more on the sign above
the entrance to Alex Feinstein's grocery. Several minutes later we jolted to a stop in front of the store, jump-
ing out, pushing our way past the people gathered at the
door. As soon as we entered, I saw Alex. He was lying
on his back beside the cash register. The white apron
was a bright crimson over his chest. The wire-rimmed
glasses hung by a single loop across his face. An ambulance attendant was kneeling beside him checking for
vital signs. I knew without asking that Alex Feinstein was
dead. His wife was sobbing uncontrollably against her
oldest son's shoulder. She looked at me. "He gave him
the money! He gave him the money! Why did he have
to shoot?" she cried. Two black women came forward
from the crowd that had formed and helped the boy
lead Mrs. Feinstein into the back room.

Franklin said something to me, but I didn't hear him.
I stood there staring at the merchant's body, still dazed
by the unreality of what I saw. I looked around the
store. The peanut-roasting machine gave off its familiar
aroma from behind the counter. A Coca-Cola sign still
flashed on the wall.

"Doc," Franklin said firmly, grasping my arm. "Doc,
come on! There's nothing you can do. We've got two
witnesses—give me a hand."

We began talking to a fifteen-year-old boy and a
woman who had been in the store when it was robbed,
trying to get enough information on the suspect to put
out a description to the other units that would now be
crisscrossing the streets around West Allison and Ford.
What did he look like? What was he wearing? Which
way had he run when he left the store? What kind of
gun? The men from Homicide and Robbery arrived,
went about the tedious business of asking more questions, while technicians processed the scene for bits of
physical evidence that might eventually connect a particular suspect with the crime.

"Why would anybody kill that old man?" Franklin said after we left the grocery and drove off. "I talked to one of the Robbery dicks just before we left. We've got a real good description on the guy. They say he's a parolee named Billy Ashe who pulled that stickup over on Lee last night. It shouldn't be too hard to pick him up."

"Pick him up?" I said as I turned to my partner. I could feel the rage rising inside me. "I hope one of us gets a chance to shoot the sonofabitch!"

As we drove away I thought about all the men like the merchant's killer that I had interviewed in my counselor's office at Soledad Prison, men who had robbed, beaten, raped, murdered other people. They had always looked so harmless, sitting there in freshly pressed denims. And the crimes themselves, like their victims, had long since been reduced to little more than printed words on a page. That was the way I had been used to dealing with crime—as data, as abstractions. That is the way judges, jurors and correctional officials, all of whom enjoy the luxury of confronting crime and criminals retrospectively in an antiseptic environment, are used to dealing with crime. It is the police officer alone in the entire criminal-justice system who is forced to witness the actual ravages of violent crime. So the victims become real people to him, as they also do to ambulance attendants and hospital emergency-room personnel.

The moon still shone brightly in the sky. The radio continued to surge with activity. Another call. We rushed toward a silent burglary alarm on Washintgon, only to find that a shopkeeper had failed to set the device properly when he had locked up for the night. Then on to direct traffic at an intersection that was quickly flooding from a water-main break. Then the emergency tone again. Another armed robbery, this one at the Mayflower Liquors on the north end of our beat. We had just checked back in service when we received another call, a familiar one.

"Two Lima Ninety-five . . . check a report of an

elderly woman wandering around in the city utility lot at Fifteen-hundred Shattuck," the dispatcher said.

Franklin and I looked at each other and smiled. "Mary," we said almost simultaneously. I turned the car around and headed for Shattuck Avenue. Sure enough, there was the unmistakable silhouette of Mary's tattered cloth shopping bag and cane on the other side of a Cyclone fence. The old black woman—she must have been close to a hundred—was well known to every policeman downtown. Scarcely a week went by when she wasn't found roaming about in some part of the city by a patrolman, much to the distress of the great-granddaughter who cared for her in a two-story house on State Street. Mary was known to have gotten halfway across the city on several of her more successful forays before someone called the department to report a "suspicious person."

"Taxi, Mary?" I called out as I pulled to the curb. Her faced brightened as she looked at us through the fence, the single tooth in her lower jaw gleaming.

"Mary, how in the devil did you get in there?" Franklin said as we walked up to the fence.

"Lawd, I dunno," she said. "Kin you get me out?" After several minutes of searching around the fenced perimeter, we finally found an open gate through which she had apparently wandered inside.

"Headquarters . . . Two Lima Ninety-five will be transporting one female," Franklin said as he stretched to read the odometer in front of me. "Beginning mileage is ten thousand nine hundred eighty-seven and five tenths."

I smiled to myself. It was a carefully followed departmental policy for patrolmen always to give their beginning and ending mileage whenever a female was transported. The procedure, coupled with the times logged by the girl in communications, was intended to protect us from accusations of rape or sexual misconduct. It seemed a peculiar formaility, though, in Mary's case.

"Mary, you're getting too old to roam around like this," Franklin said. "You could get hurt."

"The Lawd looks after me," she said placidly. I was never quite sure just how senile Mary really was. It had occurred to me more than once that she was probably the only person in the city who didn't have to pay for taxi service. We dropped her off at home and checked back in service.

"I'm ready for a cup. How about you, partner?" I asked Franklin.

"Amen," he said.

I glanced at my watch. Only one more hour, I thought. Then some other poor bastard would be stuck with Ninety-five for a while. I started thinking about Alex Feinstein again and caught myself. It was no good to do that. Angie was right. You couldn't let things get inside you. Once that began to happen to a man, it was the beginning of the end for him as a policeman. Ulcers. Heart attacks. Divorce. Nervous breakdowns. Alcohol. I had seen the statistics years before, but now I understood them for the first time. I had two or three drinks before I went to bed almost every night now. I promised myself I would have only one tonight. We sat in a restaurant sipping our coffee.

"I'll miss Feinstein," I heard myself say.

"Yeah, me too," Franklin said.

The emergency tone sounded on the portable radio. "Headquarters to Two Lima Ninety-five . . . "

"Not again!" I said as Franklin acknowledged.

"Two Lima Ninety-five . . . a fight in progress at the Tip Top Club . . . Two-thirty-four Valencia . . . no closer unit in service at this time," the dispatcher said.

"Valencia? That's way the hell and gone over on Seventy-nine's beat," I said as we left the restaurant.

We were within several blocks of the club, siren and lights going, when the emergency tone sounded again. "Headquarters to Two Lima Ninety-five . . . be advised that the fight in progress at Two-thirty-four Valencia is now a stabbing." I pushed the accelerator to the floor and a few minutes later we skidded to a stop in the Tip Top's dirt parking lot. Franklin grabbed a slap-jack off the dash and I jumped out with the heavy metal flashlight I now invariably carried. I found myself already panting with anxiety as we reached the bar's front door, wondering why I was still such a coward after all this time. We burst inside just as a large white man with curly brown hair threw another man against one wall.

"He cut a guy!" a woman shouted hysterically as she pointed at the large man. He turned and faced us as we rushed forward. I was conscious of the sound of Charlie Pride's voice coming from a jukebox in one corner as we grappled with the man and fell with him onto the sawdust floor.

"Don't take all night, Doc," Franklin shouted. He locked a forearm around the man's throat as I fumbled with my handcuffs. The handcuffs snapped shut and we pulled the man to his feet. I heard a low moaning sound. Another man was propped against the side of the jukebox, the blood from a wound over his right chest soaking the orange sports shirt he wore. "Suva-bitch! Suvabitch!" he kept muttering drunkenly as I tried to stop the flow of blood.

"Mister, you're under arrest for assult with intent to commit murder," Franklin said to the handcuffed man as an ambulance crew entered the bar. He took a small printed card from one of his shirt pockets and began reading aloud. "You have a right to remain silent. You have a right to—"

"Who do you think you're talking to, boy?" the curly-headed man said. His lips twisted into a cruel smile.

"I'm talking to you," Franklin said. "I'm trying to give you your rights, so shut up and listen, okay? You have a right to have an—"

The man spit in Franklin's face. The saliva glistened brightly as it ran down the side of one cheek, and laughter sounded from the recesses of the bar. The black policeman said nothing. I saw his jaw tighten as he looked at the man. He took out a handkerchief and slowly wiped his face.

"Okay, fine, forget your rights," he said quietly.

"You don't talk to me, nigger! You understand that, jungle bunny?" We pushed him toward the front door as a back-up unit arrived.

"Two Lima Ninety-five to headquarters. We'll be en route to the jail with one prisoner," Franklin said once we were inside the car. The backup unit would collect information necessary for a report while we booked the man.

We rode along in silence for several minutes before the man in the back spoke. "Hey, you!" We both turned sideways. "No, not you. I'm talking to the nigger there! Yeah, you, coon!" He leaned forward and pressed his face against the wire mesh separating us. He smelled strongly of sweat and liquor. "Hey, tell me something, boy! Does it make you feel real big arresting a white man, huh? Maybe make you feel like you was a man instead of a nigger?"

Franklin lit a cigarette and picked up the mike. "Headquarters, advise Two Lima Seventy-nine that Two Lima Ninety-five will be standing by at the jail for report information when they're back in service from Valencia."

"Ten-four, Two Lima Ninety-five," responded the girl in communications.

"Hey, boy! Why don't you come back here and take these cuffs off me? Then we'll see who's the man and who's the nigger!"

"Shut your mouth!" I said over my shoulder as I drove.

"Hey, boy . . . what's the matter? Cat got your tongue? Say, didn't your mammy learn you to answer when a white man talks to you, huh?"

Franklin drew deeply on the cigarette and rested one arm out the window.

"No, I don't guess your mammy taught you much," the prisoner said. He kicked the metal cage hard with one foot.

"I told you to shut your mouth!" I shouted.

"She was probably too busy sucking white dicks!

That's it, huh? Yeah, sure, that's it! Your mammy couldn't find time to take them big liver lips off white dicks. Hell, I'll bet she's given me a blow job or two!" I noticed Franklin's hands tense in his lap. "Hey, tell me, what's her name? Bet I'd recognize it. Bessie? Sapphire?"

Franklin turned in his seat, breathing heavily. His teeth were clenched. "Shut up! You shut up!"

"Bet I've fucked your wife and half your sisters, too!"

Franklin pointed to an alley off to our right. "Pull in there!" he said.

"Franklin, don't let him—"

"Goddammit, I said pull in there!"

As I stopped the car, he unsnapped his service revolver and thrust the handle toward me. Then he jumped out and opened the cruiser's back door. He unsnapped the key ring from his Sam Browne.

"Hey, what the hell do you think you're doing?" the man exclaimed.

Franklin jerked him off the seat by his hair and dragged him out of the car. The handcuff key scraped against the cuffs as Franklin unlocked them and threw them on the ground.

"Wha—" the man protested just as the black policeman slammed a heavy fist into his face. He fell back against the side of the cruiser with a grunt. Bright red spots splashed against the white door panel.

"Come on, you sonofabitch! Fight!" Franklin shouted as he raised both fists. The man started to get up just as another blow drove into his stomach. I heard the rush of air as he doubled up and dropped to his knees. A third blow sent him sprawling noisily into a row of garbage cans. Lights began to go on in windows at the backs of houses down the alley. Dogs started to bark.

My partner pulled the figure to his feet, pressing his back against the car. "Come on, massa! Come on, cap'n!" Franklin said, panting. "Show dis nigger, suh! Ah wants to learn!" He struck the prisoner again and the man fell sobbing on the ground, crying out in pain as Franklin kicked him once in the side.

I could hear the sound of voices coming down the alley now. "Franklin, for God's sake!" I said as I grabbed his arm and pulled him back. "Franklin, stop it! We've got to get out of here. Help me!" I struggled to load the semiconscious form into the back seat. The look of crazed hate vanished from Franklin's face as he helped me with the prisoner. We said nothing on the way to the jail. The silence was broken only by the radio and intermittent groans and sobs from the back seat.

"Jesus H. Christ," the gray-haired jailer said as he examined the still moaning figure that we half dragged up to the booking area. The custodian shook his head. "Fellas, I've got news for you. This one's going to have to go over to General Emergency before we can take him. I'll bet he'll take a half-dozen stitches on his jaw alone." He studied the limp form and looked at me. "What happened?" he asked. "He resist?"

Franklin Griffin and I stared at each other for several seconds before I finally said, "That's right, he resisted."

11

SIGNAL ZERO

THE ringing of the phone slowly penetrated my sleep, and I reluctantly extended a hand from beneath the warmth of the covers.

"Hello."

"Hello, Dr. Kirkham?" a man's voice said pleasantly. I sat up in bed and glanced at the clock. It was just after 8 A.M.

"Yes?"

"Doctor, I'm really sorry to bother you at this hour," the voice apologized. "My name's Don Culp. I'm with the IAD." The initials jolted me into consciousness. IAD, the police Internal Affairs Divison. My pulse quickened. I knew immediately what he was calling about "I wonder if you'd have a few minutes to drop by the office today? I need to ask you a few questions about an arrest you and Griffin made last week. Just routine. It shouldn't take very long."

The voice was casual and relaxed, like someone making a luncheon date. After I finished talking to the man named Culp, I sat there for a full fifteen minutes. So this was it. For some days after the incident in the alley, I had worried that the man Franklin had beaten that night might file a brutality complaint. But as the days passed with no word, I had begun to believe—hope— that nothing would come of what had happened. It was done and forgotten. Neither of us had spoken of it since.

Now my worst fears had suddenly materialized. I looked up the black policeman's phone number and dialed it, waiting anxiously through several rings.

"Franklin," I said as I heard his voice. "I just got a call from the IAD. It's about the Tip Top arrest. I've got to go up there this afternoon."

"I know."

"What do you mean, you know?"

"I just got one too," he said, "from a Lieutenant Culp."

"Franklin, what am I going to do?" There was silence on the other end of the line. I heard a baby crying somewhere in the background. "Franklin, did you hear me?"

"Yeah, I heard. Just do what you have to, Doc. Do what you have to," my partner said.

That afternoon I stopped in front of a door in the police administration building marked LT. DONALD A. CULP. I hesitated for a moment, then knocked.

"Come in."

The IAD man sat sipping coffee from a plastic cup as he leafed through a pile of papers in front of him. He was a heavyset man with long sideburns and unruly hair. "Dr. Kirkham! Good of you to come," he said warmly as he stood and offered a hand. "Please sit down."

"Lieutenant," I began.

"Please, just Don," he said. "Would you care for a cup?" He gestured toward a metal pot resting on a hot plate.

"No . . . no, thank you." Why didn't he just get on with it? I wondered. Start asking me questions about what had happened that night?

The IAD man stretched and leaned back in his swivel chair, revealing a snub-nosed .38 strapped on one hip. "You know, Doctor, I've got a lot of respect for what you're doing over here. We all have. It takes guts—real guts," he said. A puzzled look came across his face. "Let's see now, what was it that I needed to ask you about? Ah, yes, the Gordon arrest," he said. He turned and opened a cabinet file drawer behind him, then began thumbing through the manila folders inside. "There's so damn much work around here lately I can't even keep track of things anymore. Gordon. Here it is." He removed one of the files and opened it on the desk in front of him, unclipping a mug shot in the upper right-hand corner and pushing it across to me. "Remember the guy?"

I looked at the face above the City Jail ID number. It took me several seconds to connect the bruised and swollen image in the picture with the man Franklin and I had arrested. One eye was almost completely swollen shut, and the color photograph revealed large areas of puffy, discolored skin on both cheeks, the jaw and the upper lip.

"Yes, sir. I recognize him."

"Please . . . please," the lieutenant said. "Just Don is fine. After all, I'm probably the one that should be calling you 'sir.' Now, I see by the report that you and Griffin charged this guy Gordon with resisting with violence, as well as assault to commit murder on the bar thing. That right, Doctor?"

"Yes."

"Uh huh." He handed me one of the papers in front of him. "Is this a copy of the resisting-arrest report that the two of you filed?" he asked.

"That's it," I replied as I recognized my own signature above that of Franklin Griffin. The lieutenant paused and opened a desk drawer, removing a small tape recorder and a cassette. He smiled. "Say, you don't mind if I tape our conversation, do you?"

"No. No, of course not."

"It's just that it makes it a lot easier for me to pull all my notes on a case together when the times comes," he said. He sipped his coffee as he pulled the record button on the machine. "You understand that you're not under oath or anything like that?"

I nodded.

"Now let's just see if this report squares with the way you remember things happening that night. It's so easy to get confused on these damn things. Hell, I ought to know—I spent enough years writing them myself."

I looked at the clock on the wall, then sat watching the recorder's spindles rotate slowly.

"According to the report," Culp said, "the prisoner began complaining that the handcuffs were too tight on the way to the jail?"

"Yes, that's right."

He frowned slightly, scratching his chin. "You didn't have the cuffs doubled-locked?" he asked, referring to a tiny metal pin on the side of every handcuff that makes any adjustment of the mechanism impossible once it had been pushed in by a key. It was a standard departmental procedure to double-lock the handcuffs of every prisoner, in order to prevent allegations of police brutality by a person who might tighten his own cuffs to the point where they cut off circulation or injured his wrists.

"No. I thought we had, but I guess we must have forgotten to in all the rush," I said. "We had a rough time getting him handcuffed in the first place."

"Now, you stopped the car and one of you went back to loosen the guy's cuffs—" Culp said as he studied the report. "Which one of you was that?" he asked abruptly.

"Griffin. Officer Griffin," I said.

"Uh huh." He paused to remove a pipe and tobacco pouch from one pocket. "Hope this thing doesn't bother you." He smiled and lit the pipe, sucking noisily on it. "Kids got it for me for Christmas. Trying to get the old man off cigarettes, you know? Now, where were we? Oh, yes just a few more questions." He turned his attention back to the report in front of him. "As soon as Griffin unlocked one of Gordon's cuffs to loosen it, the guy jumped him and a fight started. That right?"

"Yes."

"What did you do then, Professor? What happened? Just tell me in your own words what you remember. Take your time now," he said reassuringly.

"Well . . . I jumped out and tried to give Frank-lin—Officer Griffin—a hand. You know, get the prisoner back under control." I was conscious of an increasing tightness in my stomach as I went on. "We really had our hands full, I mean what with him struggling and being as big as he was." I was lying, I thought. Lying to protect another policeman who had committed what amounted to a felony assault. I had always said, had always believed, that a free society is lost once those charged with enforcing its laws begin to step outside them. Dammit, I still believed it. Yet I was lying just the same. Why?

"Did you personally hit the prisoner, Doctor?"

"I . . . I guess I might have," I said. "It all happened so fast. He—"

"How about Griffin," Culp interrupted. "Did he hit him?"

"Maybe . . . I mean, I guess we both must have hit him during the struggle."

"You guess?" the IAD man said. He leaned forward in his chair and looked at me. I looked back, knowing that policemen come to interpret the unwillingness of a man to look them squarely in the eye as a sure sign of deceit.

"Did either one of you use a weapon of any kind on him—a slapjack or a stick?"

"No."

Culp took another paper out of the folder and handed it to me. "This is the medical evaluation they made on the guy after you took him over to General Emergency," he said. "I'd like you to take a look at it."

I took the report and scanned it. "Fractured ribs . . . concussion . . . multiple bruises and abrasions on face and about head . . . lacerations . . ."

"It takes one helluva lot of resistance to justify using that kind of force," Culp said, the cold gray eyes drilling into me.

"I—"

"Look, Dr. Kirkham, don't get me wrong. I understand your position completely, the kind of spot you must be in—being over here, trying to gain the men's confidence and all. As I said before, you deserve a lot of credit." He propped one foot up on the desk and rubbed his face with a hand. "Hell, man," he said as he went on, "You think I don't know what it's like out there, the way these bastards can get to a guy sometimes, make you want to rip their guts out? I was on the bricks almost ten years before they bumped me up here." He looked at me earnestly before he spoke again. "But we can't have this kind of thing—no matter how much somebody might deserve it. Maybe once, maybe back in the old days you could give a guy lumps when he needed it, but not today! Not in this department, not with all the community pressures we have to live with— the press, the civil-rights groups breathing down our neck." His face relaxed into a slight smile. "I'm not telling you anything you don't already know, am I?" he went on.

He got up and walked across the room, poured himself another cup of coffee. "I've seen this guy Gordon's rap sheet," he said. "He's a first-class scumbag. A list of priors as long as your arm. Everything from wife beating to grand theft auto. Hell, he probably deserved everything Griffin gave him."

"I didn't say Griffin 'gave' him anything, Lieutenant."

Culp slammed a fist on the desk. "Oh, knock it off, Professor," he said. "Why don't you cut out all that 'we' crap and stop trying to be one of the boys? Now I want to know what happened out there that night! What did that guy do or say to get Griffin hot enough to beat hell out of him?"

I sat there without saying anything. The tape recorder's spindles continued to turn.

"Was it you, then?" Culp said. "Are you going to try and tell me that it was you that made the guy look like somebody worked him over with a steam shovel? You're not big enough to do that to somebody Gordon's size—not without a weapon. Griffin's an ex-boxer, for Christ's sake." He walked over and sat on a chair next to me. "Please, tell me what the guy did, for your own sake. There's a chance—a damn good chance—that this one will go to the chief's disciplinary board for review. From there it could very easily wind up in court. You could be called on to testify under oath about what happened out there." He looked at me for a long moment. Then he said, "I'm sure you realize that perjury is a felony in this state."

He let the last words hang in the air.

I looked at the IAD man, conscious that I wanted to tell him what had really happened, to tell him about the incredible abuse Franklin Griffin had taken that night before he finally lost control of himself. I wanted to tell him that there are limits to what a policeman, like any other man, can take—that the law and society ask too much sometimes.

"Sir, do you have any more questions?" I asked.

"No," he sighed. "I guess that's all for now. You can go."

Later that night I filed into the assembly room with Franklin and the others. "Attention!" The room full of blue figures stood rigidly for a few moments, then the figures relaxed, bent and sat down as the long list of names and assignments began.

"Andrews . . ." the watch lieutenant said.

"Here."

"Riding Beat Sixty-one. Channing . . ."

"Doc," Franklin said, leaning over, "I'm sorry about getting you mixed up—"

"Forget it."

"I've never had anything like that happen to me before," he said. "I've never hit a guy I didn't have to."

"Just forget it, okay?"

The lieutenant finished the roll call and then began reading the evening bulletin. "All of you in and around West Allison and the project," he said. "We just got word from intelligence that a bunch of black militants are due in town tonight to start getting things worked up for the convention protest this weekend." As he spoke, I remembered having read in the paper that various black civil-rights groups were planning to demonstrate against a segregationist organization, something called the States Rights Conference, that was planning a national convention in our city the following weekend.

"That's all we know right now," the lieutenant said, "but keep your eyes open. Intelligence says that these people from out of town aren't the nonviolent type."

Franklin drove that night as we started on patrol. I sat there for a half hour or more, not saying much of anything, still thinking about my meeting with the IAD man, wondering what would happen.

"Something's wrong," Franklin said as we turned onto West Allison.

I noticed it too. The street was virtually deserted. A number of usually busy shops and bars were closed tight. I had never seen Allison this way before at night.

"Something's up," Franklin muttered.

We spent the next forty-five minutes drifting up and down the streets, listening to the radio's peculiar silence.

"Headquarters to Two Lima Ninety-five . . ." the dispatcher finally said. It was her first transmission to us in almost an hour.

"Two Lima Ninety-five, go ahead," I said.

"Two Lima Ninety-five . . . check a report of a truck blocking the street at West Jackson and Felton."

I rogered the assignment and jotted it on our log.

As we turned onto West Jackson, I could see a man standing on the hood of a panel truck in the middle of the block, addressing a small group of people with a bullhorn.

"Two Lima Ninety-five to Headquarters," I said, picking up the microphone, "be advised we'll be out of the car in the two thousand block of West Jackson on this call." I started to reach for it and then realized that we had no portable radio tonight. The watch had been short of portables for almost a week now. That worthless Douche, I thought. Why was it that, whenever you most needed anything, it was either broken or unavailable? Franklin set the cruiser's taillights in a flash position as we parked behind the truck.

"Do you realize that white racists have beaten

you! Imprisoned you! Murdered you! Violated your
women! Trampled your rights for three centuries?" said
a mechanically amplified voice as we approached the
vehicle. We worked our way through the steadily growing crowd of people and stood in front of the man on
the truck. He jabbed the air with one finger for im-
phasis as he held the bullhorn in front of his mouth.
"How much longer are you going to let yourselves be
enslaved?" the man went on as Franklin stepped forward.

"Hey, man, I need to talk to you for a minute," he
said. He motioned for him to come down off the truck.

The man stared down at him contemptuously and adjusted a pair of tinted dark glasses. "You talking to me,
slave?" As he spoke I saw a leather jacket with a coiled
rattlesnake painted on it lying next to his feet. The same
emblem was painted on the truck's doors.

"Hey, we're not trying to hassle you," Franklin said,
"but you'll have to move this thing out of the road. Just
park it over there. Then you can do your thing. Okay?"

"Move? Why do I have to move?" the man shouted.
"These streets are black! These are our streets, right?"
he said as he turned toward the still enlarging crowd.
People applauded and shouted their agreement as
Franklin Griffin spoke again. His voice was calm but
firm.

"You're violating a municipal ordinance by blocking
this street," he said.

"Ordinance?" the speaker shouted into the bullhorn.
"Don't give me no shit about no ordinance! Go across
town and tell Whitey about your ordinances! Go bug
Mister Charley about your goddamn ordinances!"

The crowd was swelling rapidly as the man's shouting
attracted ever more people. The street was suddenly
alive with black people, pressing closer to hear and see
what was happening.

"Now, look, brother—" Franklin began.

"Brother?" The man on the truck laughed. "Don't
call me your brother, Uncle Tom! You're not a

brother! You're nothing but a slave. You're the white man's flunky!"

Franklin looked at him. "We've tried to be fair, man. Now I'm giving you just thirty seconds to put that thing down and move this truck—or I'm going to bust you!" he said.

We stepped closer to the truck.

"Everybody hear that?" the man said into the bull-horn. "The white man's boy here says he's going to bust me for speaking the truth! He's going—"

Franklin reached up and grabbed one of the speaker's arms, jerking him off the truck as the bullhorn clattered to the ground.

"Help me! Brothers! Sisters!" the man shouted as we held his arm and started toward the cruiser.

"Hurry, Doc," Franklin said.

"Pigs!" I heard someone shout. Soon others picked up the chant. "Pigs! Motherfuckers! Free the brother!" A crowd of angry black faces and raised arms surrounded us. I held onto the now struggling speaker's arm and looked at the black-and-white a few yards in front of us. Just a little farther, I thought. Just a little farther! We were alongside the patrol car's front fender when I felt an arm grab me around the neck from behind. I brought an elbow back quickly and turned just as I felt a sharp tug on the handle of my service revolver. There were other hands on me. I brought my hand down on the wrist of a woman just as she pulled the gun halfway out of its holster.

"Franklin!" I shouted.

An instant later I saw one of my partner's muscular black arms flash past me and hit the man who still held me from behind. I swung hard at the woman who was grabbing for my gun and screaming, knocking her down on the pavement. Franklin still had one arm locked tightly around the prisoner's throat. We each drew our revolvers, pointing them at the crowd and backing along the side of the car as a hail of rocks and bottles began falling around us.

"The radio! Get the radio!" Franklin shouted as a

rock shattered the black-and-white's windshield. He brought the barrel of his revolver down on the head of a youth in his late teens. I lunged into the cruiser, crawling across the seat toward the radio, kicking back with one foot at someone who was trying to grab me. I froze for a split second with the mike in my hand. My heart pounded in my ears.

"Ninety-five! Signal Zero! Signal Zero! Help!" I shouted, reaching out and punching the release button on the shotgun rack. I could hear things raining down on the cruiser's roof and the sound of Franklin Griffin's voice cursing, shouting. The weapon fell into my hands. The first shell of lethal buckshot made a hollow sound as I racked it into the chamber.

I jumped out. "Get back! Goddamn you, get back!" I screamed as I rounded the rear of the car. I raised the weapon, aiming it at the cluster of people closest to me. They began to scatter and run in all directions now as I heard the welcome wail and yelp of sirens coming toward us. I could see blue lights flashing at both ends of West Jackson, flowing onto it from side streets, out of alleys.

"Get those two," Franklin shouted to another marked unit as it screeched to a stop near the pair who had tried to grab my gun.

Fifteen patrol cars and a number of vice and detective units sat at odd angles on West Jackson in a matter of minutes from the time we put out the call for assistance. Franklin walked over to where I was leaning against the side of another patrol car. He managed a smile.

"Custer and the Indians, huh, Doc?" he said as he dabbed blood from a cut on his face.

"Custer and the Indians," I repeated. I looked at the black policeman and suddenly understood for the first time why I had lied to the IAD man.

12

JUSTICE

"WHAT did you say?" I frowned as I looked at my partner in disbelief.

"Here, read it for yourself." Franklin handed me the memorandum.

I couldn't believe what I saw on the paper in front of me. The district attorney's office had let the two people who had tried to grab my gun that night on West Jackson plead guilty to "breach of peace."

"Breach of peace?" I said angrily as we stood outside the assembly room. "Franklin, that's like saying that they didn't do anything more serious than spit on the pavement! You saw what happened out there. Those people were trying to get my gun. They would have killed both of us!"

The black man sighed and lit a cigarette as we got inside the cruiser. "What can you say, Doc? That's just the way it goes—most of the time."

I started the car. Angie was right, I thought to myself. Nobody really gave a damn what happened to us: not the courts, not the people we were trying to protect, nobody. I slammed a fist against the steering wheel in frustration. How different everything was now. How very different, I thought to myself as we pulled into traffic and started toward our beat. Only a few months earlier, "crime" and "criminals" had been impersonal abstractions to me, phenomena to be examined leisurely in light of various hypotheses about deviant behavior developed by people like myself. Not any more. Crime was a personal thing now. It had a face. It had hands, too, hands that had torn at my service revolver that night on Jackson, hands that had nearly snuffed out my life another night with a gun hidden under the front seat of a car.

I looked out my window at the darkening streets. It was absurd, really monstrous to think that I might die out here. Me. The realization that it could happen, did happen, was numbing. Professors were supposed to die gray-haired and senile in their musty offices, surrounded by books and students. Not out here. Not like this. Not in the prime of life in some dirty alley or dark stairwell. None of my past life really mattered out here, I thought. All the degrees, the academic honors, the publications and the knowledge that I had spent my life absorbing. Ninety-five, I had discovered, made us all equals. Who I was and what I was hadn't mattered in the least that night on Jackson, and it didn't matter now—it never would, out here. I was just another cop, and I had already learned that for too many people that meant being the most readily visible symbol of a hated establishment, the imagined cause of all the misery and frustration in their lives.

As I maneuvered the patrol car slowly down Allison, I could feel the sensation coming over me again, just as it had so many times before. I had been ashamed of feeling it so often during my first weeks as a patrolman, but in time I had learned that the others felt it too, even veterans like D'Angelo. Fear. Like crime, it too had become an intensely personal thing. Its faces were legion. A tight ball in the pit of my stomach as we entered a dark building on a silent alarm call. A quickened pulse as we rushed toward a "man with a gun" or an "unknown trouble" call. An indescribable and recurrent dryness in my throat as I approached a suspicious person or vehicle. Cold, moist palms. A rush of adrenaline. More often, though, it was like tonight, just a vague uneasiness that unexpectedly drifted across me like a fog as I stood putting the uniform on or started on patrol. But whatever its particular form, fear was always with me—mocking me, stalking me through shift after shift. "Hours of monotony broken by moments of stark terror, that's what being a street cop is," Frank Cagan had once said.

I looked over at Franklin Griffin. I wondered why they stayed with it, men like Griffin and D'Angelo. Not for the pay, the excellent working conditions, the accolades of a grateful public. My mind went back again to the sound-truck incident on Jackson. Again I saw the faces of the people we had arrested that night laughing at us, laughing at the whole criminal-justice system. "Justice, my ass!" I thought.

The shotgun rattled in its metal rack as we continued down the block. I remembered how I had once said that policemen should not be allowed to carry such "offensive" weapons in their cars. An offensive weapon, I thought. A screaming mob of a hundred or so people armed with rocks and bottles, that *isn't* an "offensive weapon"? The memory of that night was etched indelibly on my brain. I could still see myself standing there with the shotgun. Scared. Cursing. Shouting. "Menacing an unarmed assembly with an offensive weapon," I would once have said disapprovingly. I had learned that night that the desire to remain alive and uninjured is the lowest common denominator for every human being—including professors of criminology. I had been ready to kill, would have killed, would have done anything I had to in order to survive. For now it was *my* life that was in jeopardy, *my* wife and children who might be mourning. That made all the difference in the world.

I looked at the shotgun again. If I had fired it that night, if I had actually shot, even to save our lives—my God! The community, the newspapers, the civil-rights groups, the department's own Internal Affairs Division would have come down on me like a ton of bricks. It seemed so wrong to me, so consummately unjust, that we who so often found ourselves forced to make the gravest of human decisions in a matter of seconds should then be judged by outsiders, people who enjoyed the luxury of quantities of time in which to dissect and examine a policeman's every action retrospectively. Outsiders who had never personally experienced the crushing grip of fear, the incomprehensible climate of emotional pressure in which a policeman must sometimes act. Outsiders for whom the differences between right and wrong were always so clear.

"Doc, what say we grab a quick cup before starting our duly appointed rounds? You look like you've got the weight of the world on your shoulders tonight," my partner said. "Hey, man, forget those two that they cut loose. They'll screw up again, and we'll be around to nail their asses when the do."

I nodded and returned his smile. He was right. I was letting myself get depressed and there was no point in it. I tried thinking about the few bright spots that had appeared on our horizon recently. There were some. We had just learned the day before that the man who had filed a brutality complaint against Franklin had suddenly and inexplicably decided to withdraw it. We were both relieved. It meant that Franklin would be spared the ordeal of a long investigation, one which we both realized could lead to his suspension from the force and possibly even criminal prosecution—all because, for a few brief minutes during an otherwise exemplary career, he had let himself feel and react like an ordinary human being instead of a policeman.

The withdrawal of charges also meant that I would not face the cruel choice of either committing perjury or ruining the career of a good officer and a friend. I was thankful. Yes, we came out on top sometimes, but not nearly often enough, it seemed to me. Certainly not as often as the other side, I thought. I remembered the sound-truck incident again and felt anger coming back over me. I was sick and tired of watching thugs and hoodlums consistently twist the law to their own advantage while we continued to play by carefully defined, restrictive rules that more often than not operated to the disadvantage of society's law-abiding members rather than the criminals we apprehended. I had always been greatly concerned with the rights of offenders. Now, as a police officer, I found myself infinitely more concerned with my own rights. I found myself unable to explain to myself or the men with whom I worked why those who assault or even kill policemen are so often able to find a most sympathetic audience before judges and jurors eager to understand their side and provide them with another chance.

I tried to put such thoughts out of my mind with little success for the rest of the shift. The job was starting to take its toll on me. Breach of peace, that's what trying to kill a cop amounts to, I told myself hours later as I turned the key in my apartment door. I dropped the heavy Sam Browne belt on the floor and mixed myself a stiff Scotch and water. Breach of peace—nothing more. I sat in the room's only comfortable chair and sipped the drink as I scanned the evening paper. As I turned to the editorial section, my eyes were caught and held by the title of an article in the center of the page.

HUMOROUS BRITISH POLICE
by Sydney J. Harris

One of the great unrecognized flaws of the average American policeman is his humorlessness; he has to learn a lesson from his British counterpart, the bobby, who is actually encouraged in training for crowd control to take a humorous view—hence the far more cooperative attitude of the British public toward their police force.

I crumpled the paper with a curse and threw it on the floor. It was the last straw.

I had tried never to take advantage of my unusual position in the department. But now I was ready to do just that. The next morning I called Chief Benjamin's office and made an appointment to see him. It was the first time I had seen Benjamin since the project began.

"Dr. Kirkham," the chief said as he stood and extended a hand. "Say," he continued jokingly, "you're not any relation to the officer Kirkham who nearly caused the riot down on Jackson last week, are you?"

"Sir, I've come to ask a favor," I said, coming directly to the reason for my visit. "I'd like a transfer out of the uniform division."

Chief Benjamin laughed until his face began to turn red. "Professor, do you know you're starting to sound like a veteran? Next I suppose you'll be complaining about the hours and the lousy pay!"

"Sir," I said, not at all in a mood to appreciate humor, "just for maybe a few days. The truth is I'm tired, really tired."

Benjamin nodded. "Sure," he said. "I don't see why not. I mean, since I haven't paid you a thin dime in the three months you've been here, I guess the least I can do is grant you a transfer request. Where do you want to go?"

The words took me by surprise; I hadn't really thought about it. "I don't care, really," I said. "Just any place where I don't have to be in uniform or ride in a black-and-white."

Chief Benjamin thought for a minute. "How about Vice—the sex detail? They're shorthanded right now."

The Pussy Posse, I thought. That was how I had heard the men in patrol refer to the Vice Division's sex unit. Well, at least it would get me out of uniform for a while. "Sure," I said. "That's fine."

Chief Benjamin picked up the phone and made arrangements for me to report that afternoon. "Just show up at the Vice Division at three this afternoon in casual clothes. Sergeant Kupiszewski will be expecting you," he said.

I thanked him and left the office.

13

THE FRIENDLY FOUNTAIN

LATER that afternoon I selected a pullover sports shirt, dark slacks and a sports coat. The prospect of working in plain clothes for the first time filled me with a certain excitement. I looped the handcuffs through my belt the way I had seen detectives do. Then I stuck a snub-nosed .38 between my flesh and trousers beneath the shirt. I had bought the off-duty gun as well as the high-velocity ammunition and ballistic vest just after what had come very close to being the last car stop of my brief career. I now went nowhere—not even down the hall to the Raleigh's trash chute—without the small revolver.

I left my apartment and drove to the Vice Division. It was located in a deteriorated section of the downtown area, well away from the other organizational units. The front office was alive with activity as I walked inside. Plainclothesmen were answering phones, shuffling through files and talking to people whom I took to be either suspects or informants. Some of the officers wore rumpled colored shirts and loosened ties, while others were distinguishable from vagrants and hippies only by the guns and handcuffs at their waists. I asked a policeman with a beard where I could find the sex detail. He directed me down one of the halls to a partitioned-off office area, where I found Sergeant Kupiszewski.

Kupiszewski explained that he planned to use at least part of my week with them to crack down on homosexual activity at one of the larger city parks. "We've been getting all kinds of complaints lately about fruits in the john over at Heller Park," he said. "Trouble is, I haven't had the manpower to do anything about it. Hell, I've had everybody in the office tied up sixty hours a week on whores and porno cases all month. I can't spare two guys to hang around the damn park all day long. Besides, it's such a lousy assignment, I always wind up having to draft guys for it. Anyway, I thought you and I'd take a crack at it this week and see what we can do." He began rummaging in a cluttered desk drawer of his handcuffs.

I nodded agreement, but the thought of arresting homosexuals filled me with something less than enthusiasm. After all, it was one of those things that we criminologists call victimless crime—offenses which usually involve consenting adults and which do not appear to harm anyone or anything. I had always felt that police involvement in such things as homosexuality was both degrading and an unwise waste of scarce law-enforcement resources. Well, at least I'd get an opportunity to see the practical side of a phenomenon I'd lectured and written about, I thought.

We left the vice office and headed for Heller Park.

"Sergeant, I really don't know anything about this sort of thing," I said.

Kupiszewski maneuvered the powder-blue Dodge Dart onto the freeway and accelerated sharply. "Don't worry, Doc. There's nothing to it," he said. "Listen, by the time you leave Vice next week you'll have twenty or thirty fruit pinches. Just wait and see."

"Is there really that much of it?"

We veered off the freeway as we came to a sign marked HELLER PARK—MARINA AND FOUNTAIN.

"You bet there is. Hell, we could book fifty a day out here and still not scratch the surface. It's unreal how many there are. Sometimes I think the whole world must be going gay. . . . Vice Eight Delta Twenty-three is in service at the Friendly Fountain," Kupiszewski said into the mike.

The dispatcher couldn't suppress a giggle as she acknowledged the transmission.

"Behold the Friendly Fountain," Kupiszewski said as he pointed to a large basin where a jet of water shot high into the afternoon sky. Several families sat eating picnic lunches on the grass around it. We cruised slowly down a circular drive around the park's perimeter. It was a beautiful day. I shielded my eyes from the sun and watched a gull drifting in lazy circles above the trees and grass. A young couple walked hand in hand down one of the flower-lined paths. It looked like an unlikely place for crime of any kind, I thought to myself as I leaned back in my seat and breathed a deep sigh of relief. It was good to be out of the squalor and violence of Ninety-five. I wondered if Kupiszewski and the other men in Vice realized how lucky they were not to be patrolmen.

"When I say that fruits are easy to bust, I don't mean they can't be dangerous," he said. "You've got to watch your ass every minute with them. You can get hurt. That's why we never work the park with less than two guys."

I couldn't recall any scientific literature suggesting that homosexuals are dangerous. "Why are they dangerous?" I asked.

"Because most of them have got a lot to lose if they get caught," he said. "You'll see."

We followed the winding cement path we were on until it snaked into a raised mound of grass and bushes. From where we stood, we could see the fountain, the parking area and a row of buildings just below us surrounded by benches. The building closest to us had the word MEN painted in large black letters on its door. Kupiszewski pointed to the benches which were perhaps twenty years in front of and below us. We knelt on the damp grass and peered through the bushes.

"Now that's what's known as the meat rack out

here," he said. "A queer will usually walk over from either the fountain or the parking lot and just sit around waiting to score. Other queers will come by and check out the merchandise to see if there's anything they like. Sometimes the crazy bastards'll hang around for hours, following different guys inside the can, until they finally find somebody that's willing to make it with them. . . .

"There comes one right now," he said abruptly. He pointed to a well-dressed man in a brown suit who was walking across the lawn between the fountain and the bench area.

"How can you tell?"

"I can just tell," Kupiszewski said. "After you work fruits long enough, you can smell them a mile off. He's one. Wait and see."

The man sat on one of the benches and crossed his legs and looked around. He was a thin, bookish-looking man—a teacher or maybe a librarian, I guessed.

"Now here's the way we work it, Doc," my partner said as he crouched down beside me. "You just walk on over and sit down on a bench across from him, see? Act real relaxed and casual. Only don't do anything like smile or wink—anything that might be considered entrapment. You know all about the law on that, right?"

I nodded, suddenly struck by the absurdity of two grown men hiding in the bushes outside a public toilet.

"Sit there for a couple of minutes and then get up and walk inside the john," Kupiszewski continued.

"Do you think he'll follow me?"

"He will if he's geared."

"Geared?"

"You know—a fruit, a fag."

"Then what do I do?" I asked.

"Just lean against the wall behind the urinals and act like you're combing your hair. Be sure to stand where you've got a good view of the stalls too—you can't tell which he'll head for. Then just wait until he starts doing his stuff and—"

"His stuff?"

"You know—jacking off, exhibiting himself, making

lewd solicitations, anything that falls inside the sex stat-
utes. Got it?" I nodded. "Now remember what I said.
Don't try to take him alone. Just walk over to that window right there and lean against it when you're ready.
It'll only take me a few seconds to come down the bank
here and get inside to back you up."

"All right," I said. I checked to make certain that my
shirt was pulled out to hide my revolver and handcuffs.
I left Kupiszewski in the bushes and started down the
path to the bench area.

The man regarded me with a pleasant smile as I
walked up and sat down on one of the benches facing
him. I remembered Kupiszewski's instructions. After
several minutes I got up and started walking toward the
men's room. The man on the bench certainly didn't
conform to my image of the kind of person who seeks
sexual encounters in public restrooms. I told myself
again that the vice sergeant was mistaken as I pushed
open the door to the men's room.

I went to one of the washbasins and began combing
my hair. The room was empty and silent except for the
hum of an air conditioner overhead. A heavy odor of
disinfectant hung in the air. The door swung open behind me and I saw the reflection in the mirror. It was
him.

Nothing happened for a minute or two. Then I
glanced in the mirror again and saw the figure lean
against one wall, unzip his trousers, expose himself, and
begin masturbating in plain view. I began inching toward the frosted window on the other side of the room
as the figure in the business suit gestured me toward
him and continued masturbating.

"Police! You're under arrest!" Kupiszewski said moments later as he came through the front door with his
badge in one hand.

A look of stark terror appeared on the man's face.
"No! Please don't—"

"On the wall! Move!" Kupiszewski reached for his
handcuffs and spread-eagled the startled pisoner against
the tiled surface of one wall.

"Please don't put me in jail," the man sobbed as I searched him. "I'll lose my job . . . everything. My God, my family!"

"You should have thought about that before you came in here and started flogging your dong, my friend," Kupiszewski said as one of the handcuffs rasped shut on a wrist.

"I've never been arrested in my life. Please, just let me go—I swear I'll never come back. I swear it!" The man's face was red and wet from crying. His eyes darted back and forth frantically in their sockets like a trapped animal's.

As a patrolman, I had arrested people for things as serious as armed robbery and even murder but had never gotten this kind of reaction. You'd think we had just charged him with plotting to assassinate the President, instead of a misdemeanor. I soon found out why. The man was a fifty-thousand-a-year executive vice-president in one of the city's oldest and most respected financial institutions. The arrest, if it became known, would ruin him. We walked him in handcuffs toward the car as he tried to lower his face to avoid the stares of people in the park. I felt like doing the same thing. For all that had happend to me in Ninety-five, I had never been part of anything as degrading and personally repulsive as the enforcement activity in which I now found myself involved. The man renewed his sobbing and pleading as we stood by the vice car, waiting for a marked patrol unit to transport him to the jail.

"Tell me something. You got any kids?" Kupiszewski asked as he lit a cigarette.

"Three. One of them's just a baby," he said. "Please—"

"How would you feel if one of your kids walked in there and saw a guy beating his meat, huh?" my partner said.

"I—"

The vice sergeant turned toward me. "There were a couple little kids starting in the door back there right after I saw your signal. I just caught up with them in time." He stared at the prisoner with a look of disgust on his face.

My initial shock at apprehending someone from such a walk of life would diminish in the days ahead as we arrested other businessmen, teachers (one of them a teacher of retarded children), an architect, a minister, a certified public accountant, even a psychiatrist. Indeed, I would leave my short tour of duty as a vice officer never really understanding why people who had spent their lives struggling for economic and social success would risk it all for a few moments of perverse gratification in a public toilet.

"Okay, here comes another one," Kupiszewski said, once we had turned over our prisoner and returned to the bushes that served as our observation point. "Just go ahead and work this one the same way," he said.

I looked at the tall figure that stood leaning against a metal rail behind one of the park benches. "You've got to be kidding," I said.

"What do you mean?"

"What do I mean? Look at the size of that guy!" I guessed that the man, who wore faded blue jeans and a red sports shirt, must be close to six foot three and weigh well over two hundred pounds. "I'm not going in there alone with somebody that size! Not on your life! No way!"

"Come on now, Doc. There's nothing to it. Don't worry. I'll be right outside waiting for your signal."

"I'll tell you what," I offered. "*You* go inside and be the bait this time and I'll back you up."

Kupiszewski shook his head. "I can't. I've busted him before. He'd make me right away. Besides, you don't really look like a cop, Professor."

"Thanks a lot," I said.

The man was now resting one black boot on a park bench and scratching the stubble of beard on his face as he looked around.

"Hell, I wouldn't let anything happen to you, Doc. I mean you're probably the only Ph.D. I'll ever have on my squad." Kupiszewski grinned.

"Well—"

"Come on, Professor. Let's nail him."

I repeated the routine of sitting on a bench for several minutes and then walking into the men's room. The big man followed me inside almost immediately. But the experience of having been arrested before had apparently made him cautious. He watched me as I stood combing my hair at the washbasin, but did nothing. After several tense minutes I walked out and worked my way back to the bushes.

"It won't work—I think he knows I'm a cop!" I said as I knelt on the grass next to my partner.

"Not a chance!" Kupiszewski insisted. "How the hell could he know you? You've never worked out here before. He's just being careful. Go on back inside."

"So what am I supposed to do," I said testily, "stand there combing my hair all afternoon?"

"Tell you what. He's probably just waiting for you to make the first move, so this time you walk over to the pisser and stand there with your worm out—"

"*What?*"

"Shhhhh! Quiet or he'll hear us!"

"I'm not going to do anything like that!"

"Take it easy," Kupiszewski said. "I don't mean entrap the guy or anything like that. All you're going to do is just stand there like you were John Q. Public taking a leak. That's all. Nothing improper or illegal about that, right?"

I thought for a moment.

"Now just stand there for a while and I guarandamn-tee you he'll do or say something to give us a case," Kupiszewski said.

"What makes you so sure?"

"Jesus, just look at the sonofabitch! He's been in and out of there three times since he got here."

The big man had emerged from the building.

"Now, Professor, that is what we in the police profession call a clue." My partner raised three fingers. "In this kind of setting it can mean only one of three things: Either the guy's got the weakest damn kidneys in the world, or he's got dysentery, or he's queer as a three-dollar bill. Look, there he goes again."

We watched the tall man stand and walk slowly back inside the men's room once again. This time I followed him at a distance, glancing over my shoulder every few seconds toward the bushes where Kupiszewski was watching. As I walked in, the giant was leaning against a wall blowing his nose. I stepped to one of the two urinals and stood there pretending to use it, staring at the wall in front of me. After several seconds I heard footsteps as the man positioned himself at the urinal next to me. I could see him watching me. The giant seemed about to say something but stopped as the restroom door swung open. A man came in with a small boy and waited patiently while the child used one of the toilets and washed his hands. Eight years of college and four degrees, I thought. Was this what it had come to?

The door had no sooner closed behind the man and the boy when the giant spoke. "Nice day, ain't it?"

I started slightly. "Uh—yes, yes it is." I kept him carefully in the corner of one eye as I stared at the wall.

"You come here very often?" He cleared his throat loudly and spat in the urinal.

"No. Today's the first time I've ever been here," I said truthfully.

The man next to me appeared even bigger now than he had outside. I suddenly felt vulnerable without either a nightstick or my flashlight. I had lost the familiar sense of confidence that a policeman's uniform somehow inspires in him, the feeling of being up to whatever challenge he might have to face. It also dawned on me that for the first time in my short career as a policeman I was completely on my own in an enforcement situation, and I realized how much I had come to depend on the presence of strong and experienced partners like D'Angelo and Griffin.

"Man, it sure is hot in here," the giant observed.

"Uh huh." I turned sideways now and looked at the yellowing teeth behind the man's beard. I could see that he wore a small gold earring through a pierced lobe.

"You from around here?" he said.

I shook my head. "No, upstate."

"My name's Gary."

"Uh huh."

Just then I heard a sound and turned my head abruptly away from the giant toward the door. Even my short experience as a patrolman had left me wary of any noise behind my back, and Kupiszewski had cautioned me that muggers often hung around the park men's room for the purpose or preying on homosexuals. As I craned my neck for a view of the door, it happened.

The giant's hand glided across to the urinal in front of me and grabbed my penis.

I have no conscious memory of doing anything during the next several seconds, but the next thing I knew I was standing there with one hand clamped across the back of a hairy wrist. My .38 was in the other.

"Let go of me, you faggot sonofabitch!" I shouted. I thrust the muzzle close to his face.

The giant's eyes dilated with fear as he jumped back with both hands up. "Don't shoot! Please! Don't shoot!" he cried. "All I've got's two dollars and a watch. Here, they're yours, mister! Take them!" He dropped his hands and began fumbling frantically with a watchband.

"Get your hands back up," I ordered as I stepped back a good three feet. Only television policemen remain within reach of suspects they are holding a gun on. Every police recruit learns in the academy just how easy it is to have someone snatch a gun out of your hand before your brain can command your index finger to pull the trigger. I remembered how Sergeant Quinn had once stood with his back to me and his hands raised while I held an inoperative gun against his uniform shirt. He instructed me to "fire" the instant he moved. Much to my surprise he spun around and wrenched the gun from my hand before the hammer was even partway back. In my initial shock, I had already made the mistake of getting too close to the giant with the gun, and I wasn't taking any more chances.

"Okay, get over there. Hands flat on the wall, feet apart," I said.

"Please don't kill me!"

"I'm not going to kill you. I'm a police officer and you're under arrest for . . . well, for whatever the charge is for grabbing someone—" I blustered. I kept the revolver trained on him as I reached for my identification with the other hand. Then I remembered that I had left my badge case in the pocket of my jacket which was locked in the car. "Listen, I don't happen to have my identification with me just now, but I *am* a police officer and you *are* under arrest."

"Please, just take the watch. It's worth—"

"I don't want your goddamn watch. Don't you understand, this isn't a robbery." I reached back under my shirt and pulled out my handcuffs. He looked relieved and put his hands against the wall—reasonably sure, I suppose, that I wasn't going to shoot or hit him over the head while his back was turned.

I backed over to the window and signaled Kupiszewski. A few moments later he came through the door. "Dammit, I told you never to take one of these guys by yourself. You should have waited for me."

"Yeah? Well, just how am I supposed to wait for you when this ape's got hold of my . . . my—"

"Oh."

We left the men's room with our second prisoner and waited for a marked unit to transport him. A few minutes after the patrol car left we were back in the bushes ready to go to work again. It was amazing. The steady stream of deviants visiting the park men's room was not slowed in the least by the fact that black-and-whites were now coming and going like taxis every half hour or so as we made new arrests.

"You know something, Doc, I think there may be a real future for you in this." Kupiszewski chuckled as we walked to our car late that afternoon with the day's last prisoner. The man was a sixty-year-old deaf mute who had passed me a note in which he had written, *Do you want to suck?* Unable to find any other way to commu-

nicate effectively with him, I had finally borrowed his
pen and written on a piece of toilet paper, *I'm sorry—
police—you're under arrest.*

"No thanks, Sarge. I think I'd just as soon take my
chances out on the streets," I replied as he started the
car and we left the Friendly Fountain. To this day, I
still hate the disinfectant smell of public rest rooms.

14

HIGH ROLLER

AFTER working the fountain for almost a week, I was more than ready to return to patrol. Kupiszewski and I had made some twenty-six homosexual arrests at Heller Park over a four-day period. It was not hard to feel sorry for these men. Many of them pleaded pathetically to be let go. Some wept. A few of the more desperate offered us money. It was a dirty job and I was eager to be free of it.

I was just getting dressed for my last tour of duty with Vice when the phone rang. It was Kupiszewski. "Doc, listen, don't come in until around nine tonight," he said, "and wear a suit and tie."

"Why? What's up? Aren't we working the park this afternoon?"

"No, we've got a whore trap set up for this evening. I thought you could stand a little variety—that is unless you'd rather work the fruits again?"

"No!"

"Okay, just meet me at the office and I'll run the whole thing down to you."

Later that evening at the office, I listened attentively as my partner outlined our plans for the night.

"We've got a bunch of high rollers who've been working out of some of the better downtown hotels the past few days, real class places like the Seville and the Towers," he said.

"A high roller is a prostitute, I take it."

Kupiszewski nodded. "These are broads that trick for maybe a hundred, hundred and fifty bucks a shot. Really sharp looking. You'd never think one of them was a whore if you ran into her on the streets. Most of these gals work a regular circuit around the country. They'll hit, say, Memphis, New Orleans, Dallas, Jacksonville, Atlanta, then shift to another part of the country. Some of them just free-lance, but most of them work with pimps. They usually plan to arrive at a hotel about the same time as a big convention, maybe a legislative session."

"How do they operate?" I asked. The only exposure to prostitutes I had had so far was limited to the streetwalkers on my beat.

"Oh, different ways," he said. "In the case of the hotel circuit, a pimp will usually make contact with one or more of the bellboys as soon as his girls check in. Then the bellboy will refer guys to him in return for a piece of the action. Whenever you've got bellboys, you've got whores too." Kupiszewski lit a cigarette. "That's one of the oldest laws of the universe," he added, unlocking a metal cabinet and removing a file. "Now here's a fairly typical high roller. Sally Beckwith." He opened a file and handed it to me. There was a mug shot of a strikingly attractive girl stapled in the upper left-hand corner.

I studied the picture. Very early twenties, I guessed. Wispy blond hair. Fine features and high cheekbones. A fresh, pretty face, like something out of a college yearbook. There was none of the hardness I had grown used to seeing in the streetwalkers of Ninety-five. The booking number the girl wore on a chain around her neck seemed somehow terribly incongruous.

"Sally works the big hotels pretty regular. We've busted her several times. Her specialty is parties for businessmen," Kupiszewski said.

"Parties?"

"Yeah." He laughed. "Some of them get pretty kinky. Like she's got this act with a damn French poodle. For a hundred bucks she puts dog food in her snatch and then the mutt eats it. Weird, huh?"

I was approaching the point in my brief career as a policeman where very little shocked me anymore. I was becoming numb in the special way that policemen become numb from regularly confronting the extremes of human depravity. As Kupiszewski continued talking, I recalled a man Angie and I had once arrested for burning his infant son's genitals with the glowing tip of a cigarette.

"Most high rollers keep trick books like Sally here," he continued. He opened a small brown-leather address book and showed it to me. "See, it lists regular tricks in each city and how much they're worth. A lot of it is in code. Like this one here." He poitned to the initials "CB-1" just above an address on one of the pages. "This means that this cat CB is good for a hundred bucks. And this one here is seventy-five. Here's a two-fifty! The girls usually won't give each other the names of their johns, but they will trade information on which hotels are best to work, which bellboys to see and so on."

Kupiszewski dropped the book on the desk and shook his head. "You wouldn't believe the names we find in these things—judges, politicians, disk jockeys, you name it. And just about all high rollers also keep diaries on their johns. How good this guy was. What he liked, and so on. I'm sure there are lots of people in this town who'd give a fortune to get their hands on what's in here."

He replaced the file on Sally Beckwith and locked the cabinet. "Now about tonight," he said as he leaned back in his chair.

"What are we going to do?" I asked.

"You, Professor, are about to become a john."

"Well . . . " I sighed. "That has to be a step up from posing as a homosexual."

"We're going to try working the Towers Hotel. I've got you a reseravtion there tonight. You'll just check in under your real name, using your true identity. University professor and all."

"No disguises or phony identification?"

"No, it's a good rule, any time you're working in undercover vice, to lie as little as possible and only when it's absolutely necessary. You start telling too many lies and you'll trip yourself up. On a sex detail, that may mean just losing a bust. But in something like narcotics, it can cost a guy his life. Most of these people aren't dumb. You know all about George Kirkham and about being a university professor. So stick with that."

I nodded.

"While we're at it, you better give me your gun and ID now."

"What for?"

"Like I said, these gals are professionals. You may not look like a cop, but one of them still might feel you up to see if you're carrying a gun. And they know that most of us carry two wallets—one for the badge and the other for money and credit cards. They'll feel for that too while they're cuddled up to you talking trash in your ear. Do you have your keys in your pocket?"

"Yes."

Kupiszewski held out his hand. "Just in case you get absentminded, Professor, and happen to pull them out, better take the handcuff key off the ring. Believe me, a hooker will know what that is in a hot second."

He walked across the room and removed a suitcase from a closet. "This is filled with clothes—couple of suits, shirts, ties. There's also a shaving kit. The kind of stuff any guy who's traveling would carry. Just put things away like you would in any hotel room once you check in."

Next he took an envelope from his top desk drawer and began counting out twenty-dollar bills on the blotter between us. "Now you count it for yourself and check the serial numbers against the list I've written out. Then sign for it right under my name."

"Marked money?"

"Right. Keep it seperate from your own cash. You want to be sure and use the right bills if you connect." He snuffed the cigarette out and went on. "There's a big business convention being held at the Towers day after tomorrow. We hear that some of the girls are already in town and starting to work out of the hotel lounge in the evening, you know, just picking up a few fast bucks until business gets going. Now that's where you come in. Most of us here in Vice are pretty well burned over there, but you're a new face. You should be able to operate with no trouble."

"What do I do?"

"Well, once you get checked into the hotel, just go on down to the lounge and sit at the bar for a while. Pick a spot where you've got a pretty good view of things, and order a drink. Then just sit tight and wait for a chick to hit on you."

"Should I order liquor?" I asked. I was still conditioned to the regulation strictly prohibiting patrol officers from drinking any alcohol while on duty.

The Vice man smiled. "Doc, if you go in there and order a Shirley Temple, that just might tip everybody inside that you're not—shall we say—the average bar patron, don't you think? Now I don't mean for you to get so loaded that you can't work. That's happened before!" He grinned. "Once you get approached, just be careful as hell what you say. Entrapment, you know," he warned. "Let her do the propositioning. Remember, you're just a fun-loving professor in a strange town looking for a little excitement. Get her to do all the talking."

"Suppose she propositions me. Then what do I do? Arrest her for solicitation?"

"Hell, no! The courts won't accept anything like that these days. We have to have more than that for a good case."

"So what do I do?"

"Once you score, chances are she'll want you to go on up to your room and she'll follow you in a few minutes. That's usually the way it works. I'll be sitting in the lobby reading a paper, so just nod as you go past and I'll know to follow once she goes up."

"What are you going to be doing if I get one inside the room?" I asked.

"There's a stairwell just outside your door. I'll wait in it until I hear her go in. Then I'll come out and listen at the door."

"And what do you want me to do once she's inside?"

"I was just about to get to that. The most important thing you've got to do is to make sure she actually takes the money. That shouldn't be any problem. Most of them want the cash out front before they'll do anything. Only don't act too eager. You might spook her," he cautioned. "Once she accepts the money, wait for her to start getting undressed. Then just ease over to the door and say 'all right.' That'll be the signal. I'll be standing right outside and once I hear that, I'll come in and we'll make the bust. Okay?"

"Okay."

"Oh, one other thing," Kupiszewski added as we started for the door. "These honeys usually aren't the violent type, but watch yourself just the same. She could have a blade or a gun in her purse and get real upset if she thinks you're the heat. Some whores are crazy as hell."

I nodded.

About an hour later I checked into the hotel. After I had unpacked, I took the elevator to the cocktail lounge, sat at the bar and ordered a Scotch and water. There were only a few people seated around the dimly lighted room. The only women in the place were sitting with other men, and none of them really looked young or attractive enough to be what Kupiszewski had referred to as a high roller. Perhaps there weren't any working out of this particular hotel, I thought to myself. No matter. I sipped the Scotch, concluding then and there that this was by far the best assignment I'd had since becoming a policeman. I relaxed and sat listening to a female vocalist across the room. The next half hour passed quickly and uneventfully. I ordered a second drink and after it was gone sat trying to decide if I should intensify the warm glow that was coming over me by having another. I recalled Kupiszewski's warning not to drink too much. This was great, really great, I thought to myself as I sat munching peanuts and listening to music.

"Gin and tonic," said a female voice to my left.

I turned and saw a woman in her late twenties with shoulder-length brown hair slide onto a barstool two spaces from mine. She was well dressed. The dark blue skirt and flowered blouse nicely complimented a fair complexion. As I glanced over and caught her eye, she lit a cigarette and smiled pleasantly. The bartender placed a drink in front of her.

No, not her, I thought to myself. I turned slightly, noticing how the tightness of the blouse accentuated the ample breasts beneath it. Probably just waiting to meet her date or her husband, I thought, some guy named Duke or Rollo who's around six-six and three hundred pounds. Ex-marine and insanely jealous. I sipped my drink and turned my attention back to the music. I couldn't help wondering what my wife would think of me doing this kind of work. I knew she'd be less than ecstatic.

"Say, can I borrow your ashtray?" said the woman's voice softly. There was a smile behind it.

I reached quickly for the ashtray and nearly dropped it. Easy, clod, I told myself. Try to act cool. "Sure."

"Here, we can share it," she said as she got up.

I was about to tell her that it was all right because I didn't smoke when she moved her drink to the stool next to mine.

"You staying here in the Towers?" she wanted to know.

"Yes, I am." I reproved myself for the Jack Webb tone I heard in my voice. I'll bet I have COP written all over me, I thought anxiously. "Are you staying at the Towers too?"

She smiled and shrugged her shoulders. "Ummmm.

Maybe. I'm not sure yet." A pair of shapely legs dangled from the barstool as she spoke. The short skirt had slid back far enough to reveal contoured thighs. Well, if you're going to do participant-observation research, you have to be observant, I assured myself.

We chatted casually for some minutes, during which I explained that I was a university professor in town on business. I avoided giving out any other personal information, for I recalled Kupiszewski's warning about lying unnecessarily. She told me that her name was Kay and that she was a model in town for a fashion show. Just as I was starting to believe that she might be telling the truth, she leaned close and rested one hand gently on my arm.

"You want a date, George?"

"A date? Uh—well, what have you got in mind?"

Why had I said that? I thought. That's just the kind of thing a vice cop would say. Any experienced prostitute would know that asking a man for a "date" was too vague to be a crime, and that I was trying to draw her into making a clear solicitation.

She stirred her drink and sat running a manicured fingertip around the edge of the glass. "What do you mean, what have I got in mind, Georgie?" She smiled. She suspected now. I could see it in her eyes.

"Uh—well . . . " I stammered. "Oh, I don't know, I just sort of wondered what—"

"Look, you're a nice guy and I really like talking to you," she interrupted. "But I don't have all night. Now, do you want to go up to your room or don't you?"

"Oh, sure. Yes," I said enthusiastically. I guessed that my bumbling-professor manner had convinced her, at least for the moment, that I was what I purported to be. Well, why not? I wondered if I should ask her, at this point, how much money she wanted, but decided I shouldn't. The solicitation was still too vague. Asking if I wanted to go up to my room was still too nebulous for a solid case. No, I would let her bring up the subject of money. I already knew only too well how a skilled de-

fense lawyer could turn facts around to an officer's disadvantage in court. After asking my room number, she
told me to go on up and she would follow in a few minutes. I paid the check and started to leave.

"See you soon, Georgie," she said invitingly.

Kupiszewski returned a quick glance of understanding and nodded slightly as I passed him in the lobby
and headed for the elevator. Back in my room I became
a nervous wreck. I looked around. Things didn't look
right to me and I felt certain they wouldn't to her either.
I had told her that I had been staying in the hotel for
several days, yet the room's appearance clearly contra-
dicted that. The soap and towels were still neatly in
place, and a check of the clothes in the closet revealed
that they obviously belonged to a far larger man. I wondered if prostitutes checked such things. I wasn't going
to take any chances. I set about making the room look
more lived in, scattering some towels about, uncovering
the bed, turning on the TV and so forth.

I started as I heard a knock at the door. "Who is it?"

"Kay," a voice replied.

I opened the door and she stepped inside. "You
didn't have any trouble finding the room?" I said awkwardly.

She said nothing but walked over and draped herself
across the bed, propping her face in one hand as she
looked at me and frowned.

"Is anything wrong?" I asked.

"Yeah, there is one little thing that's bothering me,
now that you mention it, Georgie."

I wished she'd stop calling me that. "What's that?"

"You'll never guess what this friend of mine that's a
bellboy here told me," she said. She turned over and
put a pillow under her head.

"What?"

"He told me that you, Georgie-porgie, are a cop,"
she said, and she looked me squarely in the eye.

"*Me?* A cop?" My heart jumped into my throat. I
could feel every feature of my face betraying me.

"C-O-P, Georgie, as in 'cop'!"

In my state of shock, I somehow managed to laugh. "That's a good one! It really is," I said as I pulled up a chair and sat next to the bed. "I ask you, Kay. Look at me. Do I look like a policeman?"

Uncertainty flickered across her face.

I stood up abruptly and walked across the room. "You said you don't have time to talk all night. Well, neither do I," I said. "I thought I knew what we were both up here for." If I had been an experienced vice officer, I would have known that prostitutes often test potential "johns" with such lines, and that if she had really suspected me of beind a policeman, she would never have come up to my room in the first place.

"Georgie, baby, don't get angry with me," she said petulantly. "Come over here and sit down, honey."

I walked over and sat on the bed next to her. I was still making a show of being offended.

"Hey, I'm sorry," she said then, "but a girl has to be careful." She brushed one shoe off with the toes of her other foot, then reached up and ran the fingers of one hand slowly through my hair. A gentle, disarming touch. The blue eyes stared up tantalizingly and the long hair cascaded over the sides of the pillow. Her lips were parted slightly.

The world's oldest profession, I thought to myself. It suddenly occurred to me how futile this kind of law enforcement activity really was. Arresting every prostitute in the country wouldn't stamp it out, not as long as men are willing to pay for the pleasure women can offer.

"What do you like to do?" she asked. She smiled impishly and pressed one finger against my lips.

"Oh, nothing in particular, really," I said as I felt my heart quicken.

She fidgeted with the top button on her blouse, slowly, calculatingly. "Well, a hundred dollars covers anything in particular, Georgie," she said.

Bingo! I thought, remembering that I still had to get her to accept the marked money. "A hundred dollars is a lot of money, Kay," I said. I shook my head and sat back in the chair.

"Oh, but you're buying quality, Georgie." She smiled as she ran a stockinged foot slowly along one of my thighs. I felt sure that I already had probable cause for an arrest, but I remembered Kupiszewski's instructions. Get her to take the cash and let her start undressing first, he had said.

"All right, I guess it's worth it." I shrugged.

"Listen," she said, "why don't we get the money thing out of the way right now, honey? Then we can just relax and take our time. Okay?"

"That's fine with me." I took out my wallet and began removing the marked twenties.

"You hands are shaking, Georgie," she observed. She drew both knees up and wrapped her arms around them as she studied me.

I laughed nervously. "Well, I've never done this sort of thing before. I mean, I'm a married man—"

Sixty, eighty, a hundred dollars. I counted the bills slowly into her hand.

She smiled and started unbuttoning her blouse. It was off in an instant. She was taking off her bra by the time I had gathered my wits enough to speak. "I'll just get a . . . a quick drink of water before we get started," I said, heading for the bathroom and thinking what a stupid thing that was to say. I emerged with a glass of water just as she began unzipping the back of her skirt. I backed over and leaned casually against the wall near the door as I watched her.

"All right!" I said loudly.

She looked up and then smiled as she slipped the skirt off. "Well, I certainly hope so," she said.

"All right!" I said again, this time clapping my hands together in feigned excitement. My voice was louder now and I stood closer to the door. Still nothing. Where the hell was Kupiszewski?

"All right! All right! All right!" I shouted as she kicked the panties off and draped herself across the bed

au naturel. She must think I'm some kind of maniac, I thought.

"You're really *all right,* Kay! You know that?" I said animatedly. I began pacing the floor. "I mean really *all right!* Yessir!"

"Well, why don't you come over here and find out for sure?" She smiled, rolling over on one hip. She brushed the hair back from her eyes and looked at me.

"Right!" I said. I started toward her and then stopped abruptly.

"What's the matter?" she asked.

"Did you hear that noise?"

"What noise?"

"Kay, I think there's somebody outside in the hall. Shhhhh! I'd better check." I stepped outside just as Kupiszewski came panting down the corridor.

"Sorry," he gasped as he ran up to me. "You won't believe this, but the goddamn elevator I was coming up on got stuck. I had to run all the way up from the fifth floor!"

Kay screamed and pulled the bed sheet up in front of her as we both came through the door together. Jack the Ripper and his crazy brother, she must have thought.

"Police officers! You're under arrest!" Kupiszewski puffed. He flashed his shield and then dropped into a chair, breathing hard.

"Well, I'll be damned," she said after several moments of silence. She got out of bed and walked over to me with anger flashing in her eyes, still stark naked. "You *were* a cop, Georgie. You lied to me! That's not nice, you know that, you sonofabitch?"

"Sorry."

Kupiszewski told her to get dressed, while I began advising her of her constitutional rights. I searched her purse and told my partner that I couldn't find the marked twenties I had given her.

"Come on now, Kay. Be a nice girl," he said. "Give us the dough, huh? We'll just have to search the damn room, and if you've got it in your box, the matrons will find it when we get to jail. Be a doll now," the vice man urged.

"Go to hell!"

Kupiszewski gave her a cigarette and spent several minutes talking in the same reassuring voice I had heard him use with homosexuals in the park. Kay finally relented and handed over the money. Then she began crying and I felt like a perfect swine. The Judas Iscariot of johns! I was soon to discover, however, that our efforts had been more than worthwhile. A key in her purse led to a motel room across town and to the arrest of her pimp, an armed-robbery fugitive from Miami. Kay herself turned out to be not such a nice girl after all. She had a long list of prior convictions for shoplifting, forgery and prostitution—not to mention several outstanding traffic warrants.

The next night I was back on patrol again and glad of it. I had decided during my week as a vice officer that whatever frustrations the blue uniform had to offer, they were nonetheless preferable to the business of trying to regulate human sexual behavior.

I was happy to learn that Angie and I would be riding partners once again, since Franklin Griffin had just started a two-week vacation. My first night back in the patrol division was like old times, riding next to the big Italian, listening to him curse and complain about everything from the tyranny of Sergeant Bernard to the cruiser's poor shock obsorbers. The days and nights following my return from Vice passed quickly now. Too quickly, for I knew that my brief career as a policeman was drawing to a close with the approach of the next quarter at the university. I had already received a call from my dean and had assured him that I would be back on campus in time for student registration and classes. I should be glad, I told myself. Being a cop had to be the most frustrating, thankless job in the world! If I had learned anything during the past months, certainly it was that. Still, I found myself overcome with an inexplicable sense of depression each time I thought of leaving. For some reason, it was hard to imagine myself doing once again what I had spent my entire professional lifetime preparing for. I tried to visualize myself standing behind a podium describing to my classes the things I had seen and been a part of out here, trying to communicate the meaning of crime from a policeman's standpoint. I wondered if I could, if anyone really could.

I turned to my partner one Wednesday evening as the two of us started on patrol. "Angie, I'm leaving. Tonight's my last night," I said.

"The hell ya say!" he exclaimed.

"I'm already packed. I turn in my gear and drive home tomorrow."

He turned the black-and-white north on Washington, and we rode in silence for several minutes. "Well, why the hell didn't you say something? We could have got the guys together and had a real going-away," he said finally.

"I don't know. I guess I just didn't want to make a big deal out of it." I began copying a stolen-car bulletin that was coming over the air.

The Italian shook his head. "Doc, you can't leave now," he said. "You been around too long. It's in your blood. I can tell. Take it from me, you'll be miserable as hell if you quit. There's nothing sorrier in the world than an ex-cop."

"Dammit, Angie! I'm not a cop. I'm a professor."

He laughed. "Maybe you was when you first come over," he said, "but you ain't no more. You're a cop, all right."

Maybe he was right, I thought to myself. Maybe I had actually become what the uniform I wore proclaimed me to be: policeman. An inexperienced one, probably even an inept one, but a policeman just the same.

I was suddenly distracted from these thoughts as I looked out the window at a darkened parking lot off to our right. "Hey, make the block," I told my partner as I turned in my seat and looked back over one shoulder.

"What you got?"

"Looks like a couple white guys parked out back of the Raven."

He made a turn at the next corner and headed back without saying anything further. We both knew well enough what the sight of white men around the notorious ghetto bar meant. Drugs, probably. Maybe whores. Either way, it meant trouble just looking for a place to happen. A failure to handle the situation now could very well mean a robbery, assault, or even a homicide call a few minutes or hours later. We eased into the Raven's parking lot as our headlights fell across a light-colored Corvette containing two white youths in their late teens. Angie put the cruiser in park and we got out.

"Hey," I said as I tapped on the driver's window and motioned for him to roll it down. He shot me a contemptuous glance and then turned away to light a cigarette.

I tapped again.

"Yeah, what do you need, man?" he said irritably as he cracked the window an inch. The throb of rock music blared from the car's interior.

"What are you guys doing down here?" I demanded. I shone my light on the front seat.

"I don't think that's any of your business, Officer."

"Okay, let's see some identification."

"Why?"

"What?" I said as I leaned closer to the car.

"I said *why*," the youth repeated. "Why should I have to show you any identification? We're not doing anything. Besides, it's still a free country."

I sighed. Now let's not counter-aggress, said a voice inside me. The professor's voice. "Look, son, I'm going to give you the benefit of the doubt. Maybe you two don't realize just how bad an area you're in," I said. "All we're trying to do is to keep you from getting—"

"Hey, Burt!" The driver laughed, turning to his companion. "You believe this? The man's concerned about our welfare!" He turned up the radio.

"Get out of the car!" I snapped.

"Why don't you just fuck off, man! You've got no right to hassle—"

I opened the door and grabbed the driver by the front of his shirt. "I said out of the car, shithead!" I shouted, jerking him off the front seat. The two top buttons on his shirt popped off in the process. "Now let's see some ID," I demanded, pressing his back against the side of the car. He began fumbling with a wallet. I snatched the license out of his hand and stood there examining it.

"All right, Theodore. Now listen up!" I said as I handed it back to him. "It's been a rough night and we'd kind of like to get through it without coming back down here to work a goddamn killing. So I'll tell you what: You two come back some other night to score your dope or your whores. You can get your heads caved in then. Just not tonight, okay?"

The driver stood there with his lower lip quivering. "You won't get away with this," he said. "I'll file a complaint! I'll have your badge!" I looked at D'Angelo and returned his grin.

"You wouldn't want it, asshole," I said. "Believe me, you wouldn't want it. Now get in that car and get out of here before you talk yourself into jail!"

The Corvette's engine fired, and a few moments later its taillights disappeared down the block.

"Doc, shame on you!" Angie said. "It's cops like you that give us all such a bad name."

"Shut up."

"Ya know something," he began as he unwrapped a fresh cigar and lit it. "I been thinking. Maybe if you was to get yourself a little education, it might help you 'relate' to people like that a whole lot better."

He chewed on the cigar as we both started laughing.

It was the only time on that last night as a patrolman that I found anything to laugh at. As the final hours and minutes ticked away, I began to realize just how much a part of my life the badge and all that went with it had become. I knew that I would miss it, but I couldn't for the life of me understand why. I very nearly turned back on my way to sign the resignation papers the following morning. Maybe just a little longer. . . .

15

HOMECOMING

"I am the resurrection and the life: he that believeth in me, though he were dead, yet shall he live."

A gust of wind furled one corner of the flag, exposing the polished mahogany of the casket beneath it.

"And whosoever liveth and believeth in me shall never die," the minister continued. A member of the honor guard stepped forward and adjusted the flag with a white-gloved hand.

A woman in her early twenties sat crying almost inaudibly on one of the folding metal chairs beside the casket while an infant pulled at a strand of beads around her neck. A second child of three or four stood beside her and stared around uncomprehendingly at the crowd that had assembled on the damp morning grass. A year. Had I really been gone that long? I wondered as I stood in one of the rows across from Ron D'Angelo and Franklin Griffin.

The minister folded the book in his hands and stepped back.

"Present arms!" a seargeant's voice commanded. The figures in blue saluted as the honor guard drew their service revolvers and fired three volleys into the air. There was silence for a moment, and then the sound of a lone trumpet in the distance. Taps.

The woman clutched the baby tightly as someone bent and put a hand on her shoulder. I looked at the

casket. I had never met the twenty-four-year-old patrolman. He had started at the academy as a recruit just
after I left the department and had had less than nine
months on the force. Now he was dead and his partner
was in critical condition. Both men had been shot down
two nights before as they responded to an "unknown
trouble" call on Beat Ninety-one which turned out to be
an armed robbery in progress. I looked at the casket
again as the final notes of Taps drifted across the field
and the blue rows held their salute. I felt a thickness in
my throat as the tears began welling involuntarily in my
eyes behind the sunglasses. It was strange to be crying
for someone I had never even met. Perhaps I cried for
myself, because I realized that it could just as easily
have been me there beneath the flag, my family beside
the casket. As I looked around, I realized that every
policeman there must be thinking the same thing.

After the service was over, I walked slowly across the
lawn with D'Angelo and Griffin. We said nothing as we
stood watching the long line of cars with flashing blue
lights wind its way out of the cemetery.

Later that day I sat in my office back at the university, thinking about the funeral and all the things that
had happened during the past year. I was a policeman
again. I guessed that I had never really stopped being
one, not even after I left the force. Angie had been
right. The job had gotten into my blood. Something
about the life I had known during those months had
made it hard to readjust to the life of a university professor.

I pushed a pile of ungraded term papers to one side
of my desk and stared out the window. I had learned so
much about other human beings, so much about myself
on the streets of Ninety-five. Even as I left the beat, I
had sensed how much more there was to be learned in
the street laboratory that I had only glimpsed as a
rookie patrolman. In my study of crime, I was frus-
trated at the prospect of being confined to the class-

room after my return. This frustration led me to join the police force in our local community a few months later, to work without pay in my spare time as a uniformed patrolman. Before long I found myself leading a Jekyll-Hyde existence of an even more intense sort than I had known during my months in Ninety-five: By day, I did the same things as any other university professor—lecturing to classes, advising students, attending faculty meetings, serving on committees; by night, however, and on weekends, I was back in a blue uniform once again—mediating family fights, writing traffic citations to irate motorists, handling drunks.

While it made for an unusual and sometimes exhausting life, I came to relish it. As a patrolman now in an essentially middle-class community, I discovered a whole new range of law-enforcement issues and problems as I went about the business of policing suburbia, problems that I had not known in Ninety-five's black ghetto. I was also on my own now, working a one-man patrol unit and forced to make decisions without the reassuring presence of a Griffin or a D'Angelo. My continued involvement in law enforcement seemed to lend a fresh vitality to my criminology lectures, as I found myself able to relate formerly abstract concepts and theories to things I now actually experienced. I felt that students were coming away from my classes with meaningful knowledge.

My role as a professor-policeman also made it possible for me to make some practical contribution to the field of law enforcement itself. Returning to campus, I remembered all too well how little training I had received in the police academy to prepare me for the job's enormous human challenges—the countless daily stresses and ethical pressures that went along with the badge. With a number of other policemen I set about producing a series of training films aimed at preparing patrolmen for the interpersonal problems they must confront. Our efforts proved worthwhile. Today that film series—which re-creates incidents experienced by

myself and other officers—is being used in the training
of police officers in all fifty states, as well as at the FBI
National Academy.

While my decision to continue working as a police officer after my return to campus was a personally valu-
able one, it made for some professional difficulties. The
idea of a junior professor of criminology directing
traffic at accident scenes and breaking up bar fights
proved upsetting to a few of my senior colleagues.
Doing such outlandish things hundreds of miles away
was one thing, but to be doing them literarally in the
shadow of the university was something else altogether.
Then, too, there was the matter of my sudden departure
from what was considered by some as a "sound" or
"proper" academic perspective. Since my return from
Ninety-five, I had begun making statements in the
classroom which bordered on ideological heresy for an
untenured criminology professor. I told my students
that I believe we academic criminologists have let ourselves become far too remote from the realities of the
crime we seek to understand and describe. I said that
just as I would not seek the professional advice of a
physician who had never personally examined and dis-
sected a human body, I felt it was equally unwise for
society to turn to "armchair experts" in its search for
answers to the problem of crime. Some of my comments
on the need for dramatic reforms in the nature of both
criminology education and research were blunt. A great
many university criminologists would not know a criminal if one bit them in the ass, I told one class. (I blame
my prolonged association with D'Angelo for the indeco-
rous nature of that remark, although I stand by its validity.)

My ongoing work as a police officer, coupled with
the changes in my views as a criminology educator, began to elicit grumbling from a handful of traditionalists
on the faculty, and complaints about my new orienta-
tion being unseemly for a university professor. The
writing was on the wall. I felt the first official repercus-
sion late one spring afternoon just before the end of

classes, only a few days after I had received a federal grant which would allow me to spend the coming summer months working as a full-time narcotics officer in another large city.

I was called in by the chairman of the faculty personnel committee and told that my performance as a professor was considered less than satisfactory. Yes, he knew that the committee had been most enthusiastic when it hired me, but they were badly divided on my case now. No, there were no specific complaints about the quality of my teaching and research—beyond the fact that I was devoting too much time and effort to applied research and not enough to producing articles in scholarly journals. No, no other professor on our faculty was being given a negative evaluation. Only me. I just didn't seem to be "working out." I wasn't showing the kind of academic potential the committee members had thought they saw in me when I first joined the faculty. He hinted that unless there were changes in the immediate future, I could look forward to a similar evaluation the following year. My failure to win promotion and tenure would eventually mean my automatic dismissal under university regulations.

I reconciled myself to the possibility of having to leave the university sooner or later. Yet all around me I could see signs of change. I was not the first to venture outside the walls of academe. As I was getting ready to begin work as a policeman in Ninety-five, Dr. John Coleman, a distinguished economist and the president of Haverford College, had left his campus in search of the meaning of work in contemporary America, a reality from which he felt he had become too remote as an academic. He roamed the country for several months working as a ditchdigger, dishwasher, cook and garbage collector. At our College of Law, a senior professor took a leave of absence to work as an assistant district attorney, prosecuting cases for the first time in his life after years of teaching the law in theory. Within my own School of Criminology, I discovered that there were a number of professors who agreed with me that practical research in our discipline was long overdue. Included among these was our dean and another junior professor who had just applied for a grant that would permit him to pursue his interest in criminal investigation by working full-time with a police detective division. Perhaps the old ivory-tower ideal was crumbling faster than I imagined. I hoped so. I had spent most of my adult life preparing to teach college students, and it was the thing I did best.

"Dr. Kirkham."

I turned toward the youth who stood in my doorway.

"Sir, could you please sign my class schedule for next quarter?" he said.

Sir. It still seemed a little strange being talked to like that even after all this time. I couldn't remember many people calling me sir during my months in Ninety-five. I scratched my name on a piece of paper and glanced at my watch. Only a few minutes to class. As I began to gather my notes my eye was caught by the title of a book lying on my graduate assistant's desk. *The Super Cops*. There was no such thing as a super cop, I said to myself as I started down the hall. Cops were men like myself, just a lot of ordinary men.

I walked into the classroom and stood for a few moments surveying the faces in front of me. I spread my lecture notes on the podium. "Today we're going to continue talking about the police and society. . . ."

Here are the facts.

The conclusions are up to you.

These books?
Fiction.
Keep telling
yourself that
as you read.